The SUPERSTARS

GW00385149

The Superstars was watched by an average of over 14 million people during 1976.

It is television's most popular sports series, watched by more people throughout Great Britain and Europe than any other. The total audience for the 1976 series reached an estimated 300 million people.

To Mandy

The SUPERSTARS

David Vine

AIDAN ELLIS

Acknowledgements

Kevin Keegan cycle accident pictures by kind permission of John Hawken, Evening Post, Reading.

Photographs on pages 29, 31, 33 and 37 are used by kind permission of Peter Hylton Cleaver.

Photograph on page 31 is used by kind permission of Ron Pickering.

Photograph of Bjorn Borg on front cover is used by kind permission of Le-Roye.

Photographs on all other pages are used by kind permission of the BBC.

"The Superstars" is the Trade Mark of Candid Productions Inc.

The author would like to acknowledge the assistance of Trans World International (U.K.) Inc.; Ian Smith, BBC Producer "The Superstars"; Stan Greenberg (Biographical Research) and Ron Pickering.

The views, observations and opinions expressed in this book by the author, David Vine, are of a personal nature and are not necessarily those of the British Broadcasting Corporation or Trans World International (U.K.) Inc.

ISBN 85628 057 7
© David Vine 1977

First published in 1977 by Aidan Ellis Publishing Limited, Cobb House, Nuffield, Henley-on-Thames, Oxon.

Photo set by Stevenage Printing Limited, Stevenage, Hertfordshire.
Printed in Great Britain by Garden City Press Limited, Letchworth, Hertfordshire.

Contents

INTRODUCTION

Madison Square Garden in New York, is filled to what the organisers and promoters love to call "capacity". To be more exact, 19,500 people are in there. Outside they tell us that 300 million are watching the scene inside "The Garden" on worldwide close circuit television. And in England, where it's the middle of the night, just short of 100,000 patrons, have paid £300,000 for the privilege of sitting in selected cinemas.

"My Lords, Ladies and Gentlemen, Mr. Joe Frazier, the heavyweight boxing champion of the world, the holder of the richest prize in sport, is about to fight Mr. Muhammad Ali." And he does. And he wins. It is March 8th, 1971.

Two years later *Sports Illustrated* magazine is on the bookstalls. The page 20 headline over the lead story shouts: YOU GOT TO HAVE A GIMMICK. And they found one in a 26,000 acre community surrounded on three sides by water, just two miles from the Gulf of Mexico.

Joe Frazier is getting ready to compete again, surrounded by officials, sponsors and spectators, but not a boxing ring is in sight. There *is* a golf course — and plans for six more. One for each day of the week. There's a cycle track where Frazier has been having trouble working out the intricate mechanical details of a three-speed gear; a swimming pool where he's just dog-paddled fifty metres in just short of two minutes, twice coming close to drowning on the way. And there are seven other sporting stages where Frazier is aghast by the sight of his rivals — nine of them — doing rather better.

Sports Illustrated calls it all ". . . . a not-so-real decathlon." On BBC 1, Great Britain later watches an edited American TV recording as part of the Easter Monday holiday Grandstand. In commentary, I call it "some of the most unusual competition in sport". It is April 23rd 1973.

Three years later, November 17th 1976, BBC 1 is transmitting what has become one of the most popular series on television. Shaun Usher, TV critic of the Daily Mail, has said, in headline form across five colums: THEY'RE PUTTING THE FUN BACK INTO SPORT. Britain's world light-heavyweight boxing champion, John Conteh, uses slightly different words as he hits the finishing line of a 600 metres Steeplechase in 1 minute 41.2 seconds.

As he almost collapses, I thrust a microphone at him, and ask him what he now feels about competing against the rest of Europe. Conteh glares at me. I'm sure it's a glare. His lips have got that bluish tinge, his eyes just ever-so-slightly rolling as if for once he's failed to dodge an opponent's right.

Four — or was it six — body racking, chest-heaving sighs later, the Liverpool boxer sums it all up.

"This is no longer a joke. . .it's. . .it's bloody serious!"

"*It*" is The Superstars. This book is what I saw, what I heard, what I reported and commentated on — and a bit more!

Why, how and when
Rotunda, Florida, USA 1973

"Colin Bell of Manchester City is the fastest footballer in the country and Malcolm Allison has always said Belly's about the best athlete in the business. Calls him Nijinsky.'. . ."

"Rubbish. Channon's faster than Bell. . . ."

"Maybe so, but I'll bet half a dozen rugby threequarters could beat the lot of them. . . ."

"Have you ever seen David Hemery lifting weights? For his size he's amazing. He's built like a beanstalk. '. . ."

"But what's the point of putting Bell, Channon or any of your rugby men against a sprinter, or matching Hemery with that great fat Russian weightlifting giant Aleksey whatever-you-call-him? It's obvious who would win."

"Jonah Barrington, the squash player is a bit of a fitness fanatic isn't he? Wonder if he's as fit as Hemery. . . ."

And that last snatch of conversation was nearer to reality or a contest, than anything else that had been talked about. It became reality, or at least a contest, in the United States, forty miles south of Saratosa, Florida, early in 1973. Richard Button, who'd twice won the gold medal in figure skating in the 1948 and 1952 Winter Olympic Games, was the man who put it together. With the assistance of commercial sponsors and the American Broadcasting Company, ten stars were taken to Rotunda, a relatively new development of living and leisure, a city in the round (no trouble in giving it a name).

Some of it was built, looking like a slice of an orange, the rest was on a plan. And with Florida already claiming more golf courses than any other state in the Union, Rotunda decided that one of the priorities of the whole project was—a golf course.

"How about a couple of courses? There's going to be a lot of people living here when we've finished it all. . . ."

"Or perhaps three . . .? Or what about the guy who's retired and does nothing else but play golf. He doesn't want to play the same course every day. . . ."

In the end, the perfect solution was reached. The Sunday course, the Monday course, the Tuesday course, the Wednesday. . . . Finally, there were seven. You daren't take a day off from leisure.

The ten stars had two days to prove what they could do. Who was the best? The Superstar? And if it wasn't just pride and that natural competitive element, how about the prize money—122,000 US dollars and a few bonuses flying around to be picked up as well. Just to make sure there was always something to aim for, even when your chance of winning looked as far away as the possibility of Muhammad Ali admitting he wasn't good enough (but that wasn't his reason for not taking part), there were 300 dollars for every point you won in every event.

The events, for America, didn't take a lot of choosing. The mixture of popular sports, those that would provide spectator appeal and test the ability of the competitors: swimming, lawn tennis, cycling, golf, ten-pin bowling, 100 yards sprint, baseball hitting, table tennis, the half-mile and weightlifting. The problem of the run-away victories was solved by barring the specialist from competing in his own sport, and each man had to enter only seven of the ten events. That basis, with one or two amendments has stayed with The Superstars ever since.

So they came, or were brought, to Rotunda. And the essential ingredient — Names — was there, from baseball to tennis, from boxing to skiing.

Rod Laver, "the greatest tennis player the world has ever seen" (you could just argue but most would agree at the time): says Laver, never the most expressive extrovert," I suppose they'll expect me to win the table tennis but I haven't played this ping pong business in ten years. And as for bike riding. . . ."

Joe Frazier, the man who'd beaten Muhammad Ali but now was just a few weeks on from having lost his world title in just two rounds to George Foreman in Jamaica: "I'll win the weightlifting. Ah can do 'bout 300 pounds. Don't know about the ten-pin. . . Ah can hit 'em okay, ah juss can't keep the damn score."

Jean-Claude Killy, the triple gold medal skiier: "I'll have a word with Laver about the cycle racing. There's a lot of technicity involved. . . ."

And there was Bob Seagren, like Laver rightly being called another world's best, this time "the world's best pole-vaulter". Every time Seagren looked at the prize-money board festooned with dollar signs and noughts, he flashed what one writer called "an acre or so of white teeth" and grinned. Seagren had never taken part for money before in his life.

Add to that list six others all with their own army of fans, either on site or away, awaiting the outcome of it all.

"O.K. Superstars, Gentlemen, can we have you for event one, the heats of the swimming race. It's 50 metres, two heats and then later on there'll be the big 100 metre final. . . ."

Killy, Frazier, Seagren and racing driver Peter Revson (later tragically killed in a car accident) line up on the pool side.

"You O.K. Joe?"shouts one of the handlers as he notices the first of what are to become a succession of wrinkles appearing across the big man's forehead.

"Yeh, ah guess so. I can swim fine but are you sure there's a shallow end here somewhere with sumpin' for me to grab hold of?". It was pre-fight nerves, or sumpin'.

Half a minute or so later Revson, Killy and Seagren hit the finish. There was nothing wrong with their performances for openers. Everyone heaved a sigh of relief as they realised it wasn't going to be a horse opera and the stars were out for the money; they were serious.

Almost as an afterthought, Revson, Killy and Seagren, together with the judges looked back up the pool for the fourth man in this first heat. Frazier was just about to make the turn in the twenty-five metre pool. Somehow he managed it back again, but it was a dog paddle! Official time 1 minute 42.5 seconds, which one statistician quickly pointed out was just about double the time set up by Johny Weissmuller, the original Tarzan, when he won the Olympic gold medal in 1928. But he'd swum twice as far as Frazier!

Revson eventually won the 100 metre final and if you go back far enough, his time of 1:18.2 would have won an Olympic gold medal. Seagren was second and really from that moment, the pole-vaulter never looked back.

He won the cycle race (where Frazier got cramp, Johnny Bench the Cincinatti Reds baseball player broke his handlebars and Jean-Claud Killy taught Rod Laver the "technicities" so well that Laver beat the skiier into second place); he slaughtered Frazier in the weight-lifting; and took the baseball hitting and the half-mile to win the Superstar show with 49 points, 21 ahead of Killy in second place.

Seagren's teeth flashed again when somebody handed him just short of 50,000 US dollars, his first ever sport pay cheque for his 2-day outing. But Seagren had proved a point—behind the laughs, the man who'd trained to adapt his accepted skills and techniques to "foreign activities" had beaten the best they could find to oppose him. Behind the laughs, there'd been more than a little soul-searching as reputations began to suffer. The Superstars had worked. There were obviously "a few changes to be made" but as Joe Frazier was heard to mutter as he walked away from it all, "You don't catch me like this again—if there's a next time, it's goin' to be a different ball-game when I get in there."

A few months later, in England, we didn't have Frazier but we had "the different ball-game" the big man had forecast.

The first Magnificent Seven!
UK National, Crystal Palace 1973

Don Revie, at this time still boss of Leeds United F.C., didn't seem too happy. "Billy Bremner is a very valuable commodity."

Revie was speaking in that now familiar deep-thinking serious fashion, his chin beginning to jut and the little wrinkles appearing over the eyebrows. You have to listen to Revie. He has that way of producing words, sometimes interupted by the ill-timed pause which somehow gives him authority. You know he believes what he's telling you. He was telling us about Billy Bremner, one of his Leeds United flock, whose Scottish flair and footballing ability had made the Leeds captain one of the most effective players in the world. A man very close to Revie.

"The Don" decided to re-inforce his point, the lecture brought about by the ideas he'd just listened to, ideas from BBC Producer Barney Colehan, commentator and athletics coach Ron Pickering, the Rugby League man Eddie Waring and me.

"I don't know if I can have Bill risking his neck—and his legs—at the sort of things you fellows have been talking about," said Revie. "This commando type obstacle course one or two of you have been on about—it could be suicide." But the man who was to become England's soccer supremo made it clear that the challenge of multi-sport competition was one which sparked off something in his mind and would do the same for the players he nursed and cared for.

What we all wanted was a genuine competition—not a knock-about circus act. It happened, eventually, as a spin-off from the American programme with Trans-World International, an agency-promotional company headed by Mark McCormack of America, setting up the event and the BBC translating it into television terms. Ian Smith produced and directed it, and Ron Pickering joined me on the commentary side.

"I don't care if the prize money is half-a-million dollars. If there's another one of these don't you get me within a hundred miles of it." It was golfer Tony Jacklin on the tennis court sidelines of Crystal Palace, Day Two of the first ever British Superstars championship, late in August 1973.

Jacklin had been having a hard time and with five of the ten events gone, the former British and US Open champion had achieved only one spot of success, a solitary point from the pistol shooting. His neck hurt, he was rubbing his right arm and shoulder and was obviously thinking twenty-four hours or so ahead when he was due to defend one of his other golf titles in a home-based tournament.

"Did somebody say this Superstars business was easy?"
UK National, 1973.

The start of it all – the first Superstar event in Great Britain, 100 metres, Crystal Palace, 1973. L to R Bobby Moore, Barry John (1st), Roger Taylor, Tony Jacklin, Joe Bugner, Jackie Stewart.

"Don't you ever have anything to do with me getting involved in this again," he shouted—and was now gripping one of his advisors ("Advisor for how long?" we thought) by the tie. Perhaps it wasn't as serious an assault as it may have looked. No, it wasn't but Jacklin' wasn't the happiest man in the world just now.

Of the seven who were here for this first British title—Jacklin', Barry John from Welsh rugby, Joe Bugner the boxer, Roger Taylor from tennis, athlete David Hemery, Bobby Moore representing football—it was the seventh, motor racing driver Jackie Stewart, the little Scot, who started something. To be quite honest, I didn't have him anywhere in my top five when we talked about the possibilities the day before it all started something.

To be quite honest, I didn't have him anywhere in my top five when we talked about the possibilities the day before it all started. Hemery, Bugner and Roger Taylor were my pre-match favourites and I was quite happy with the choice when, in the first event, the 100 metres, Taylor ran a good second to Barry John with Bugner fourth. Stewart was third and provided the first magic moment (there were plenty more over the years). As they came down the 100 metre straight, the chicken-wish-bone frame of the little Scottish Grand Prix driver was shoulder to waist with the massive Joe Bugner! Bugner thought he'd inched the Scot out. Stewart, as he'd done throughout his career, and as he was to do throughout the next two days, had it right.

"Well run Joe," he said, almost as he crossed the line. "That was a good fourth place. And don't argue".

But Bugner had his revenge in the pistol shooting where Stewart was the hottest favourite you could ever imagine: a champion and international clay-pigeon shot. And despite Stewart's claims that his success in that had nothing to do with air pistols and five clay discs as targets ten metres away, nobody paid much attention to what was politely described by one of his rivals as "yet another piece of Scottish fertiliser!"

Stewart was last to shoot and had watched—and now and then coached—the rest of the field. Bugner used four shots before he broke the first of the five discs but then got the aim right and ended up with a very good score of 82 points out of a maximum 100, calculated on the number of shots used to break all five targets.

Stewart came to the firing line. Surely a formality, and the rest of the Superstars, sitting behind him, were already laying bets on whether he'd get all five in five shots. He quickly answered that by missing with his first shot.

"Well done Jackie," shouts Bugner. "Keep it up".

Stewart half-turned his head, said everything he needed to without uttering a word, and turned back to the target. Two discs left to break, twelve shots left. He's overtaken David Hemery who was lying second to Bugner, and the luckless Tony Jacklin. "Oh my God," mumbles Jacklin, head in hands. "Every time I look like making the first three, somebody does something. . . ."

Stewart misses. Then a hit. One target left. And he's got to hit it with the next shot to tie with Bugner. And the blonde curly head of Joe the heavyweight is buried behind a rather large shoulder! Stewart shoots—and the white clay disc ten metres away is still there. With the next shot he hits it. He's second to Bugner who gets slowly to his feet with hand outstretched, a grin slowly appearing across his face. Stewart turns, places the gun on the table and with shooting hand outstretched, points his finger at the oncoming Bugner.

"If I had one more Bugner, I'd shoot you!"

Behind the Stewart-Bugner head-to-head battle, Hemery the athlete and Barry John the Welsh rugby hero were quietly plugging away. Hemery won the swimming, John had got the tennis, that 100 metres and the football. Roger Taylor wasn't getting much, Bobby Moore even less. Jacklin was getting tired. But it was inside the gymnasium that the Superstars really came to life and since then it's become the hot-bed of every competition. "The crucible" as Ron Pickering calls it.

In these early days, it was a four-part test. Dips on the parallel bars where the arm must bend to produce a right angle between the bicep and the forearm, feet off the ground, raising and lowering the body until the competitor drops from exhaustion; the standing long jump; a shuttle-run, five times up and back a ten yard stretch; and then the squat thrusts, hands on the floor with arms straight, the body stretched out behind with one minute in which to bunny hop the knees up to the elbows and back—and up—and back. . . .

"We're now in the fitness emporium," was the way in which Ron Pickering introduced the event on television. From the apprehensive looks on the faces of the men who were about to have that fitness tested, Pickering might well have called it the torture chamber. And it was those parallel bar dips that provided the moments.

Stewart is on, bending the arms that have wrestled with the steering wheels of Grand Prix cars around a few thousand corners on the world's motor racing circuits. This time the arms are just raising and lowering his body. The pace gets slower. "Ten, Eleven, Twelve" is the count. Hemery is watching from the bench, looking just a little worried with his turn still to come. "Not down," shouts the judge as Stewart fails to bend the arms to that 90 degree pitch.

"You sure?" Stewart almost screams at him. "Christ. . . ."

"Thirteen, fourteen, fifteen, sixteen. . . ."

Suddenly it's very quiet and if there *is* any noise apart from the judge and Jackie Stewart, it's certainly not coming from the Superstars bench where the muscles are beginning to ache—just at the thought of what they've soon got to try and do.

On the bars, Stewart is almost gone. The dark hair wet now with sweat is hanging around his face which is beetroot in colour. There are veins standing out on his neck which I didn't know existed in the human body (but no doubt Ron Pickering with his physiological background is mentally naming every one!).

"How many is it?" whispers Barry John to David Hemery. As Stewart bends the arms yet again, the judge calls it: "Eighteen". Stewart suspended in mid-air, attempts to turn his face towards the judge. His head moves no more than half-an-inch, his body now like one lump of concrete.

"Nineteen," he screams.

And he's right. He's not only doing it, he's counting them as well. The judge nods approval.

One more and the little Scot is finished. His big but friendly rival, Bugner beats him by three and Hemery beats them all with a score of 25.

And after that if anybody had told me that it wouldn't be too long in Superstars before we'd be watching somebody not just beating that but more than doubling it—over fifty dips—I'd have just said "Let me be there to see it". I was. It happened. It comes later.

But here at Crystal Palace, it was Hemery winning the cycle race with his legs looking like a speeded-up film as he selected the wrong gear and didn't dare risk another change at speed; Bugner getting a triumph in the weightlifting and Hemery, again, despite a handicap, taking the steeplechase. That run gave him the title, the first ever British Superstar, and a £4,000 cheque. One thought as we left the Crystal Palace, and again as we watched the recording on television on New Year's Eve was. . . .

"How do you follow that? They were the stars of British sport. Where do we find seven more for next year and if we do, Hemery is bound to win."

We'd reckoned without a former pupil of St. Kevin's comprehensive school, who has eight brothers and sisters, an English mother and a West Indian father.

Belgian heat (Bracknell) 1976
Kevin Keegan on the range during his epic
2-day Superstar triumph.

The TV circus.

The Kirkby Kid moves in
UK National, Crystal Palace 1974

"They're what? Offering odds of 3 to 1 'gainst me? Well I'll tell ya, I saw Hemery win it last year and I reckon I'd 've given him a better fight than those others did, yeh? I might stroogle a bit in the swimmin'. I tell ya, I've always thought water is only thur to be walked on!"

Born Kirkby, Liverpool. Age twenty-three. Height 6 feet, weight 12st 7lbs. Bachelor. Occupation, professional pugilist. It is July 1974 and Mr John Conteh is about to attack the Superstars scene.

Those odds of "3 to 1 against" he was quoting were for real. *The Sun* Newspaper had opened what they called "a special file" with screamer-type, white on black headlines, every day. "WHO WILL BE THE SUPERSTAR" . . . . "BATTLE OF THE SUPERSTARS" . . . . YOUR GUIDE TO THE BIG TELLY CHAMPIONSHIP" . . . . Every competitor was being taken apart — Development, Present Status, The Future, His Events, His Quotes, Assessment. . . .And they'd made Conteh 3-1 with Hemery favourite at 6-4 for the 1974 title to be televised later — on Boxing Day. (And Conteh read something into that!)

The line-up was intriguing. Conteh and Hemery; John H. Stracey, the cockney boxer who, by the time the programme was televised was, like Conteh, a world champion; two footballers, Mike Channon (rated at 4-1) and Colin Bell (second favourite at 5-2); the cricketer who was to become the most controversial England captain ever, South African born Tony Greig; and a yachtsman, round-the-world sailor and ex-para-trooper, Chay Blyth (the outsider at 100-8).

"O.K., I know you fellas are having a bit of a laff about the old man here." They were just about the first words Blyth uttered after an hour or so of walking around and surveying the Crystal Palace set-up, when he arrived on the first morning.

"I may be thirty-five and 13½ stone but I'll tell you one thing. . . ." Blyth glowered at the assembled company and pointed a rather short, stubby finger at the lot of us. "It's going to be bloody hard work for me, but I think I've got a lot to offer. And another thing . . . this fella," stabbing the finger into his own rather impressive chest. . . . "this fella is not goin' to be bloody last!" And with that, the man who'd spent so much of his time alone in a boat, strode off to plan his campaign.

"Tough little sod idn't 'ee", said Mike Channon in that unmistakeable Hampshire/Wiltshire accent. "Woodn' like to meet 'im wiv football boots on!"

Hemery didn't say anything; he rarely did unless it was to consult the chart he seemed to carry everywhere and on which he'd logged his personal bests, the points he thought he could pick up, and where he might have to improve. . . . When I asked him what he thought of his chances, he dropped into that Hemery habit of pausing, then a rather shy, half laugh and said in his faultless, very polite English: "Well, I think Conteh is very fit and will obviously do well and I am rather impressed already by Colin Bell, the footballer. He could be very impressive". The Hemery chart could well have been a crystal ball.

Hemery was barred from the first event, the 100 metres. Bell, we said, must be favourite but with Channon in the line-up it was really a race to settle the argument of "who's the fastest man in football?" Mind you, there might have been a couple of other players ready to dispute that Channon and Bell were the best that soccer could provide when it came to sprinting (and we discovered a little more about that not so long afterwards) but right now, these two were going to settle it.

At the gun Channon didn't have the best start, but for Bell it was disaster. He missed his footing as he thrust himself away and must have lost a yard. Channon was away and there was really no chance for Bell to catch him as the Southampton man was well up at the 50 metre mark. Channon hit the tape and almost fell as he attempted to look over his shoulder for Bell. But the man he saw was—John Conteh. The boxer had run well with Bell third, Greig and Stracey fourth and fifth.

I was down on the track with a roving microphone and rushed over to Channon. I could have taken my time because Channon was breathless. He sank his head down beneath his knees for a moment, hands on hips and then looked up. The Channon grin was back. "What happened to Bellie? Did he fall over?"

I think he knew Bell had slipped but couldn't resist the banter.

"Well done Mike," I said, "10 good points for that win".

"Yeh, wadn't bad was it?" he gasped. "I'll need those points—I mightn't get many more."

Another prophet.

A few days before the Superstars event, Conteh had expressed some doubt about the weightlifting. "If I don't drop it on me feet I'll probably chin me'self with it". He'd managed to get some coaching and, full of confidence, he sat and watched the rest perform at the lower weights. With 65 kgs (143 ½ lbs) on the bar everyone except he and Hemery found it too much. So it was the boxer and the gold medal hurdler.

The competition was being run on what's called the O'Carroll formula (he had to be an Irishman to invent something like this). It's a system that relates the weight of the lifter's body to the weight he has to lift, in other words making it equal for all men regardless of size. Conteh was the heavier man and with both of them crowded around us as we worked with calculators, tables and scraps of paper—even the Hemery chart couldn't sort this one out—I finally came to the conclusion that Conteh had to lift 7½ kgs (16½ lbs) more than Hemery to win.

And for once, I think, Hemery made a mistake. Both of them lift 75 kgs. Hemery goes to 82½. Conteh jumps to 85. Hemery, trying to push him, decides to put more weight on the bar and hoists 87½. Conteh looks at the Hemery technique, not a glimpse of a smile on those handsome dark skinned features. There's no doubt that the boxer is struggling just a little, the science of weightlifting with the athlete, Conteh no more than a keen beginner when it comes to this. His style has been learned quickly and it's over-exaggerated, it shows when he asks the handlers to put on 90 kgs, just 1¾ lbs short of the 200 lb mark on the bar.

The lift is the clean and jerk, a two-part action where the bar is first hoisted up past the chest to rest, with arms bent, almost across the shoulders and under the chin. Then in one explosive movement, splitting the legs and crouching under the bar, it has to be jerked overhead, one movement, until the arms are straight, legs together and straight, and held there until the referee signals he's satisfied.

Conteh knows all this but over-exaggerates the movement of the split, doing it almost as if he thinks it's the right thing to do rather than to get maximum thrust and power. But it's there, 90 kgs. And this where, in my opinion, Hemery made the mistake. Instead of attempting to match that, which would have forced Conteh to lift at least 97½ kgs to win, Hemery asks for more weight, 92½ kgs. Conteh shouts across: "If he does this, what do I 'ave to do to beat 'im?"

Out with the calculator. "John, 100 kgs, 220½ lbs".

"Kerist".

Hemery approaches the bar. Looks at it, huffs and puffs a bit, quite rightly, exhaling the breath, forcing the concentration into his mind and body. "Hate the bar," is the old advice shouted by coaches to their lifters. "Hate it, dominate it."

Conteh, I'm sure, is hating Hemery just for this moment, but as Hemery lifts we all know it's not on. He's gone too far. He's allowed three attempts at any one weight.

Second try. Blyth, Bell and Stracey, long out of it, sit and watch with Stracey mentally doing it all, grimacing and twitching on his seat as Hemery tries again.

It's up to the shoulders, 203¾ lbs and Hemery jerks to bang it over his head. It's there . . . but at the last second, the arms start to crumble, Hemery's legs just won't hold still and international referee Oscar State shouts "No lift".

The third try, but Hemery now is beaten mentally and it's the same result. Conteh has been let off that psychological 100 kgs barrier and

(UK National Aldershot 1976)
J P R Williams trying to boost the spirits of fellow rugby playing Welshman Gareth Edwards on the weightlifting bench at Aldershot.

(GB heat St. Ives 1976)
The .38 FN Browning about to score another 9 for Christian Neureuther, the German skier.

steps onto the platofrm and a second later 95 kgs is stretched above his head.

It was really *that* which lost Hemery his Superstar title—and gave it to Conteh. The boxer had the luck as well—six of the most unorthodox runs scored in the cricket event off an automatic bowling machine, but some very impressive cycle racing, beating Hemery again; they shared the gymnasium tests, Conteh doing 35 dips and when it came to the final event, the steeplechase, Conteh was already the champion. Bell won this last event with Conteh second, Hemery handicapped out of it but it didn't matter. It was Conteh, Hemery and Bell 1, 2, and 3, the two men Hemery said he feared before the start of it all finishing either side of him.

But what about that other threat—Chay Blyth telling us all "this fella won't be bloody last!" He wasn't. He finished 1½ points ahead of the tail-ender, Mike Channon who, to be fair was suffering from German measles. But Blyth had another piece of good fortune, if you can call Channon's measles Blyth's luck! With some performances which were a good as he'd said they'd be (he failed to score in only one of the eight he chose)—he was allowed to compete in the rowing.

"Ah, excuse me," said Hemery, when the decision of the organisers was announced. "Are you sure that's right? After all, he just about lives on the water".

Official explanation: Blyth is a yatchsman and therefore the "barred from own speciality rule" does not prevent him from taking part in a rowing race.

"Well, I'm not the guy to interfere with an umpire," drawled Tony Greig, "but somebody seems to have forgotten this chap rowed across the ***** Atlantic ocean a few years back, so don't tell me he can't do 100 metres now!"

"Different type of boat," interjected Blyth. "Good decision". He won—but only by nine-tenths of a second from Hemery who was gaining on the "yachtsman" all the way.

Hemery of course accepted it but got the last dig in, remembering that Blyth rowed across the Atlantic. "Another 2,999 miles and I would have caught him!"

The Superstars didn't go that far for the next milestone but it did take us into Europe, bringing in the skiiers, the ice-hockey players, the Grand Prix motor racing circus, a 20 stone discus thrower, and a man who was to become an extraordinary Superstar.

(*Aldershot 1976 UK National*)
John Conteh with Malcolm Macdonald reveals his deep thoughts to the author for TV history.

(*UK National Aldershot 1976*)
Gareth Edwards and his former athletics coach, Ron Pickering "doing the chat".

Superstars goes European—and the Hemery disaster trail begins—*European series, British heat, Aldershot 1975*

Jackie Ickx got slowly out of bed in his hotel room just off the M3 motorway about fifty miles out of London. He groaned, just a little, as his feet touched the floor, not that it was cold or that the carpets were thin. It was as he went to straighten up that he realised that "all was not well", as he later put it.

Perhaps it was just one of those mornings for this little Belgian Grand Prix racing driver who had twice won the Le Mans twenty-four hour classic. Before that he'd been Belgian national motor-cycle champion for three years. But this morning, even after a shower, he didn't feel much like a champion of any kind. It was as he stood in front of the mirror over the washbasin and went to comb the dark, curly hair into some sort of order that he discovered that "all was certainly not well".

Comb in hand, the arm stopped half-way up to his forehead. Ickx frowned, looked at the arm and went to raise it again. It wouldn't move—and there was a rather unpleasant pain from his shoulder running around the back of his neck and quite a little way down his spine.

Jackie Ickx has discovered that twenty-four dips on a set of parallel bars and fifty-seven squat thrusts in one minute on the first day of the first ever European Superstar championship heat had left its legacy!

Ickx was the first of what was to become a remarkable breed of motor racing Superstars, but I suppose we should have realised that these men had something just a little bit special. We should have realised it when we saw the performance of Jackie Stewart when it all began two years ago, but at the time, I for one, just accepted it as part of the Stewart individual make-up, the Scottish blood in his very competitive veins—those standing out on his neck during the dips in particular!

But as we were to find out, the Grand Prix drivers who spend their business life wedged into a specially sculptured cockpit, lying almost on their backs and somehow controlling with hands, feet and brain what is no more than a thundering power-box of an engine and a fuel tank lashed to a set of wheels . . . as we were to find out, the Grand Prix drivers seemed to come out of the same mould.

Stewart's activities, particularly in the gym, and now Ickx's (to be followed by one or two more, including James Hunt, the enigma of it all) were of a superb standard, way and above what anyone in their wildest dreams could have expected from them. They're not muscle-men, they're not track athletes accustomed to using the muscles we were testing here. And yet almost without exception, they came good.

"I suppose it's because we live on a higher plane in some way than most other sportsmen — at least, that's all I can put it down to." Jody Scheckter, the South African driver who now lives in Spain, was talking to me about this phenomenon just before I managed to hustle him, with wife and mountains of baggage, onto a plane for Jo'burg at Brussels airport.

"You see, in our business, there's no way we can compare with some of these other guys in terms of athletics ability — on paper. But we have to keep fit and then our sport is slightly different."

Scheckter stopped for a moment, looked around him as if he was forming that picture in his mind — yet another corner on yet another race-track and if he got through it, another one looking up. And three cars in front of him, perhaps, and two more breathing and roaring down his neck. Noise, smell. . . .

"You see , if a footballer for instance, makes a mistake he's probably missed a goal — important; if a runner makes a mistake, he'll probably come second or third; a cricketer gets his wicket knocked down. If we make a mistake, we could be dead."

He didn't need to say any more — it was terrifyingly crystal clear.

Jackie Ickx, here in England for this opening of European Superstars, was in pretty mixed company. We had three footballers — Carlos Rexach, the Spanish captain from Barcelona; Bjorn Nordqvist, Sweden's World Cup captain; and Colin Bell again, who was one of the two British competitors, David Hemery the other. Bell and Hemery had been chosen to compete for Britain in this heat after their performances in the 1974 British National championship. Conteh, who'd won that was unable to take part this time due to the damage he'd done to his right hand in a non-title bout agains the American Willie Taylor in August of 1974.

However, we did have a boxer taking part, Frenchman Jean-Claude Bouttier, the former European Middleweight champion who'd knocked out Britain's Bunny Sterling in a title defence in Paris. There was also one of the famous names of lawn tennis, the jovial Italian Nichola Pietrangeli, and a hockey player from Holland by the name of Ties Kruize. The Dutchman was the top goal scorer in the 1972 Olympic tournament in Munich with eighteen goals, but to be quite honest, his name didn't mean a lot to me at first. I got to know him rather better — and so did everyone else.

For the event, we were back at the Aldershot Military Stadium with the judging etc in the extremely capable hands of the Army Physical Training Instructors. Nobody argued and there was no reason to. What a pity we couldn't have taken thešе P.T.I.s around Europe with us where some of the decisions were, to say the least, rather difficult to accept.

If there'd been a "who's the fastest footballer in Britain" battle when

Mike Channon and Bell came together in the 100 metres in the 1974 British Superstars, then we had a European argument to settle this time. Three soccer players, Rexach the Spainard, Nordqvist the Swede and Bell, all of them entering the sprint with Hemery banned.

Bell won the football argument with a time of 12.2 seconds, but he didn't win the race. That went to the Dutch hockey player, Kruize who was a tenth of a second faster than Bell, giving us the first sign that he could be a little better than I for one had thought. And it was Kruize, twenty-five years old and the son of another famous hockey player, who was involved when we moved down to the lake for the rowing.

"Are you ready?" boomed the voice of umpire Richard Burnell as Rexach, Bell, Kruize and Bouttier, the French boxer were held on the stake-boats, their single skiffs in line, with 150 metres ahead to row in this first heat.

At the gun, Bell had the worst start in lane 2, with Bouttier, beside him in lane 1, going well. Kruize had the lead but then Bell, still trying to get some sort of co-ordination with arms, oars and rowlocks, veered off course and almost onto Bouttier. The Frenchman, who'd expressed fears of the water before the start — "Eet ees only for washeeng" — went white, broke a rowlock and stopped. Kruize crossed the line first followed by Rexach, and Bell quite a way back.

Umpire Burnell went into conference. "Official decision . . ." The voice boomed again. "Official decision, all competitors will re-row, race invalid." Bell's face dropped; Kruize half-smiled, his victory now worthless; the Spaniard and the boxer were impassive.

On the stake-boats for the second time. "Are you ready?" Bell looks across at Bouttier, oars back and poised over the water. The French boxer seems to be trying to edge his skiff sideways away from Bell, understandably. . . .

"Go." Kruize has the start, pulling well in the outside lane. Bell is better this time, and Rexach and Bouttier are just about level as they come to the 50 metre mark. But suddenly "The Voice" booms again through the hand-held megaphone: "Reshacks, left oar." The command was meant for the Spanish football captain who was getting more and more off line, but if he recognised his name I don't think for a moment he knew what Burnell was talking about. And Burnell didn't risk having a go in Spanish. Bouttier, the Frenchman, obviously speaks English and obviously thinks everyone has to obey the command, suddenly pulls like a man possessed on his left side! It had to happen. . . .

Bell crashes into Rexach, Bouttier joins them and Kruize powers on to win again. Down the course, it looks like Piccadilly Circus in the rush-hour during a police strike!

Cue "The Voice", "Official decision. . . ."

(Bracknell, Belgian heat 1976)
On the range at Bisley with the man who caused more trouble for the TV commentators than anyone, Marco Ostarcevic

elgian heat Bracknell 1976)
e King of the Downhill ski slopes, Austria's
anz Klammer.

Champion Conteh in the European qualifying heat at St. Ives, beating two skiers, Duvillard (2nd) and Russi.

"Oh no," groans Bell. "I've done it twice, or one and a half times, already. If he says re-row, I'll sink."

"Official decision . . . Kruize wins and qualifies for the final. Bell, Rexach and Bouttier will re-row."

"Good-night," says Bell.

But they do re-row. Bell wins it from Rexach, and the rest was almost an anti-climax. Hemery makes the final from his heat and then wins overall with Kruize only third, Bell last of the four.

"What do I get for that?" Bell shouts across to us.

"Two points," I shout back.

"Great," is the reply. "I've only done 550 metres in this flippin' boat for that!"

And on they went. It wasn't long before it was virtually a two-man battle, Hemery versus Kruize. There was always Jackie Ickx — and Bell — not far away and those two forced a shoot-off in the pistol event, Ickx finally taking the points with a maximum ten bulls with a .22 automatic from fifteen metres.

In the gym, where Kruize opted out, only half a point separated the racing driver and the footballer after the three tests that later caused Ickx to wonder if he'd ever be able to comb his hair again! But Hemery beat both of them here, twenty-six dips, seventy-one squat thrusts and 9 metres 32 on the medicine ball throw (the third test that was to be dropped from Superstars later on).

But it was the steeplechase that provided the real story of this European opener. The tenth event, and after nine, Hemery was leading with 51 ½ points to Kruize's 49, Ickx third (29), Bell fourth (27).

Hemery had a 100 metre handicap to overcome under the "near to speciality" rule. "I might just make that up on most of them but I really don't think I have any chance of catching Colin Bell. He would probably beat me in a straight race." Hemery was, as ever, making the calculations but even he didn't calculate what *did* happen.

With that overall points situation, Kruize the Dutchman was the only man who could prevent him winning this British heat of European Superstars and automatically qualifying for the final in Rotterdam some weeks on. To beat Hemery, Kruize had to win the steeplechase or be second and ahead of Hemery. There were one or two other permutations but we discounted them as they meant Hemery not making the first three places, which even with the handicap we thought he was bound to achieve.

At the gun, the seven (Pietrangeli, the Italian tennis player, was the only man who opted out) set off, five hurdles and two water jumps ahead. Hemery, looking a very lonely figure, was 100 metres behind them and had an extra hurdle to jump. It was Kruize who set the pace out front, Bell and the Swedish footballer Nordqvist in his shadow. Hemery

(Belgian heat Bracknell 1976)
The eight at Bracknell in 1976 including the three "Ks". Franz Klammer (top left) Rudi Krol (top right) and Kevin Keegan (centre).

(GB heat St. Ives 1976)
Bernard Russi, Switzerland's Olympic ski champion.

(GB heat St. Ives 1976)
England football goalkeeper Peter Shilton tries to guage the height of the hurdles before his winning run in the steeplechase at St. Ives.

was gaining ground all the time, those long, rangy legs carrying his frame over the metres between him and the pack. He'd caught Bouttier the boxer, was up on Rexach.

As the hurdler came to the water jump we all knew there was a chance he might even catch Bell, who had now overtaken Kruize for the lead. Hemery stretched, the leading leg went for a light foothold on top of the barrier. And didn't quite find it. Hemery crashed into the water as his foot slipped away from him — and the rest of the field slipped past.

With Bouttier unable to finish, Hemery was last, Bell had won it and Kruzie had got that second place to win overall. Colin Bell with his steeplechase victory (1 min. 36.2 secs.), a really magnificient run confirming everything that has been said about him, took third place overall with Ickx fourth. But it meant that Ties Kruize was the man who'd go forward to the final, not Hemery. With a strange, cruel and ironical twist, the Dutchman, who'd won because of Hemery's crash, never made that final.

He himself crashed in a far more serious and dramatic fashion not many weeks later. In a road accient, Kruize went through the windscreen of his car and the next time I saw him he was lying in a hospital bed in Holland. One leg was suspended from the ceiling, his face was terribly scarred, a jagged piece of glass missing his left eye by a millimetre. He was well enough to talk to us and was already planning his come-back to hockey and Superstars.

"Who get's my place in the final — I don't think I'll make it," Kruize said, smiling as well as he could.

"I think it will be David Hemery as the next highest points scorer," I replied.

"I hope he will do well," said Kruize. "But not too well. It would be nice for a Dutchman to win."

With his permission and that of the hospital authorities, we brought in a film camera and battery lights and I interviewed this most likeable man about his crash and his chances of getting back on his feet, and I next saw Kruize the following year. He was back with Superstars, invited to Vlaardingen in Holland to present the trophy to the winner of the 1976 Dutch heat.

"Hi," he shouted across the lawns of the Shell centre where the event had been staged. "Good to see you again — I told you I'd be back!" He was fitter — and a lot fatter — but had a definite limp. "See you next year when I compete again — and in Moscow for the Olympic hockey." It was a nice thought.

(UK National 1976 Aldershot)
David (Hemery) telling David (Vine) "How I
won the UK swimming race".

"Never mind the Superstars out there in
France, what's page 3 of The Sun like?"

Supermac's 10.9 — *Swedish heat, Malmo 1975*

Getting there was the first problem. I was due in Sweden, Malmo to be exact, right on the country's southern tip. It was at the end of July 1975, and the day I should have been flying out with the rest of the BBC team I had to be in our Manchester studios for a recording of our sports quiz programme "A Question of Sport". There was only one solution, a charter flight.

Making the best use of it, I took the two resident quiz captains, Henry Cooper and Cliff Morgan (later appointed head of B.B.C. T.V. Outside Broadcasts) up with me, leaving Denham airfield just outside London in a Piper Seneca. Henry Cooper's reaction, when he saw the plane standing on the grass strip, was typical of the man who must be the most popular sports personality in Britain: "'Ere David my son, wot you letting us in for nah then, eh? You sure this thing knows the way?"

We clambered in and an hour and a quarter later were in Manchester, by which time Henry had decided it would be a good idea to "'ave one of these 'ere things for me'self. Easier than the motor ain't it? . . . Yeh, very 'andy. . . ."

With "A Question of Sport" completed — I think 'Enery's excuse for losing one of the two rounds we recorded that day was "jet-lag, me old son" — it was back to Manchester airport and a night flight ahead in the trusty Piper to Sweden. The North Sea and the oil rigs, at one in the morning, when you're not all that far above them, were fascinating.

We made Malmo at three a.m. — about an hour late.

At least one of the Superstars I'm sure was asleep, because there was no way he could have produced the performance he did a few hours later if he'd been out investigating the local architecture. Great Britain's "man in Sweden" and prospective Superstar, was Supermac.

"It's me that I'm worried about David, never mind anything else!" Supermac, or as he was described officially on the programme, England and Newcastle United footballer, Malcolm Macdonald, had just provided his answer to my pre-match questioning of this week's Superstars . . . "What do you fear most . . . who do you think is the man to watch. . . .?"

As he answered a grin came over his face; that face with those high cheek-boned features and narrow slit eyes that could have him mistaken for a boxer, a successful one too. Mac had been running an eye over his seven rivals at breakfast, all of them now clad in the familiar track-suits, yellow, blue, red, white, and from somewhere had come a dark brown one for the England striker.

(Belgian heat, Bracknell 1976)
The Keegan plan to stay afloat in the canoe race.

(UK National 1976 Aldershot)
David Hemery, Britain's most successful Superstar.

"Well, I've got all the gear" he said as he wandered out to the coach carrying training shoes, spikes, hold-all and a towel round his rather substantial neck. "All I've got to do now is use it!" When we arrived at the Hasthagen Stadium he did just that.

"Right, this is the lane draw for the 100 metres, can you pay attention please gentlemen . . . attention s'il vous plaît . . . "Ken Hawkes, organiser for Trans World International and a former BBC man was addressing his multi-national flock.

There were two world champion motor-cyclists, Giacomo Agostini (Italy) and Angel Nieto (Spain); a world champion speed skater from Holland, Harm Kuipers; a triple world champion table tennis player, Kjell Johansson, with the world record holder in the steeplechase Anders Garderud, both from Sweden; Willi Steveniers from Belgium, one of Europe's top basket ball players; and Macdonald. Watching from the grandstand was the eighth man, the German motor-racing star Jochen Mass who'd decided the sprint was not for him.

Macdonald drew line 4 and was in between the two little motor cyclists. We were wondering if Garderud, the tall, blonde Swede, and long-distance athlete, would show well here as he was on the outside lane. I hadn't once seen him smile and by now the grin had left Macdonald's face as well. He was prowling up and down a few yards from the start line, the weather not too pleasant.

Nieto, the little Spaniard who'd won six world titles on mini motor bikes, was looking just a little overawed by it all; now and then laughing nervously to himself and, to be fair, we didn't rate his chances too highly in this powerful line-up of mixed talent. Already a pattern was slowly taking shape—the racing drivers and the athletes were becoming the successes of the Superstar competitions. The failures tended to be boxers (with the exception of John Conteh), cyclists—and all Spaniards!

"To your marks please," shouted Ken Hawkes.

The red-jacketed Swedish starter took over, pistol ready, and the seven came to their marks. A touch of fidgeting from men accustomed to the tension of big-time sport although, in this strange environment, they were all one edge. Without exception, every competitor in Superstars is a champion of some sort, a star. Rarely, if ever, are they last, but here, every week in every one of the ten events, someone has to be. Which is why it matters to them.

As the starting pistol cracks Johansson, the table tennis champion, is a yard up. Macdonald is away well as is Kuipers, the speed-skater. At 50 metres there's only one man in it—Macdonald. And his power is quite remarkable.

Even from the grandstand you can hear him forcing the air in and out of his lungs like a compressor, arms pumping, legs driving his quite substantial thirteen stone body over the ground. It's impressive. And so

"Oh yes, these overseas Television trips really are great fun".

UK National (Aldershot) 1976
The 1976 UK National championship — and a few moments later more than one of these Superstars was under the canoe again, in rather different circumstances.

is the time on the watch as he hits the tape . . . 11.0 seconds dead. He's half a second up on the rest, Johansson the only man near him.

But there's one small problem—the start of Johansson. He obviously had a false start but wasn't recalled by the second pistol shot from the Swedish starter. It couldn't go unchecked and, despite the fact that "our man" had won it, BBC Television and representatives of the Belgian and Dutch broadcasting companies made a three-legged protest. If you're asking why, the answer is simple. The false start would have stood out a mile on television—in fact it did when we viewed a play-back on site. The event, and indeed the whole of Superstars would have lost all credibility. It had to be re-run—and we went to tell Macdonald.

"Yeh? Really? Tha's OK with me, I'll have another go. Just gettin' warmed up. . . ."

Supermac was already taking off his tracksuit, the rest glad at the chance to try and do better.

"To your marks. . . ."

Johansson again away well, but this time on the gun. Mac is with him but not for long because it's a repeat performance and the footballer is doing it again. We heave a sigh of relief—and then one of almost disbelief. The clock says 10.9 seconds, he's not only won it again, but this time gone faster.

Down on the track I interview "our star" who shows the first sign of the manner in which he was to compete for the whole two days.

"10.9? Not bad, not bad at all. Yeh, sure I'm pleased but it's for Britain isn't it—and for football!" And with that, the fastest Superstar ever, picked up his towel and wandered off towards the coach. "Right then, what's next?"

Comparisons of course can always have holes picked in them, but when we have sprinters and athletes representing us in the Winter Olympic Games as bob-sleigh crews, what price Macdonald with a bit of training as a member of our Sprint relay squad for the Summer Games?

After all, his time of 10.9 would have *won* the gold medal in the first four Olympic Games and was only three tenths of a second—as long as it takes you to win—outside the time of Britain's only Olympic sprint gold medallist, the great Harold Abrahams!

The other events were a bit of a mixture for Macdonald. No success in the rowing ("I'm going for survival, not glory"); absolute disbelief when watching racing driver Jochen Mass scoring goals in practice for the soccer penalties against the Swedish national keeper ("I can play the game and I've missed a few—but I've never hit them like he does, almost one-legged . . . and bleedin' scored!"); and then the pistol shooting.

The weapons were .9 mm army pistols (M40) and the range fifteen metres. Each man had two rounds of five shots, a bull scoring 10 giving a maximum score of 100.

All eight men took part and, between them, they shoot five bulls in the first round, Mac getting two of them to lead at the half-way stage with an excellent 45 out of 50, four up on the little Spanish motor-cyclist, Nieto. Garderud, the tall Swedish steeplechaser, was having a nightmare and making sure that everyone was well behind him—three of his five shots not even hitting the target!

Last to go in the second round, Macdonald needed 32 out of 50 to beat Harm Kuipers, the Dutch speed skater, and pick an unexpected 10 points victory. "Honestly," he half whispered to us as he went to the firing table for the second time, "I've never even held a pistol before in me life!"

Arm outstretched, and squinting down the sights, he fires, five times. The range and safety officer gives the formal command: "Unload. Mark." And the judge, with that little fairy wand-type stick they use to pin-point the holes in the target, called the shots. "Ten, ten, ten, ten . . . eight. "Two short of a maximum and Jackie Ickx's record in Aldershot, but Macdonald has shot a 93 out of a possible 100 to win.

Before I can say a word to him on the hand-held mike, he kills any thought of an appropriate first question stone dead. "David, jiss call me Jesse!"

In the weightlifting hall, Macdonald is again supreme. Despite being the heaviest man in the competition at 83 kgs, just over thirteen stone, he beats his nearest rival (the motor-racing representative, Jochen Mass) when he hoists 92.5 kgs overhead with some more of that huff-and-puff he used to such good effect on the track.

After his rowing, he wisely decided to give the water a miss when it came to the swimming (Mass again winning here), but got a runners-up place in the tennis. Back in the gym, it was Mass and Macdonald again. A gigantic medicine ball throw of 11.11 metres from Mac, seventy-one squat thrusts, but disaster in the dips, only fourteen, and he had to take second place overall to Mass in the gym.

With just the steeplechase to come, Macdonald was a point behind the German Grand Prix driver, 44 to 45. But Mass had done his eight events, Macdonald had this one left and with six men in the field (Garderud banned) and the points for the event 10, 7, 4, 2 and 1 for fifth, his chances were good. But we'd almost forgotten, or not noticed, that Kuipers, the Dutch speed skater, could win the whole shooting match, lying third with 38 points.

But Macdonald had worked it all out as well. He kept Kuipers in his sights all the way round the 600 metres, let Johansson, the Swede, run on to win and the British footballer came home third, a long way behind Kuipers, but it didn't matter.

Supermac was Superstar. "Great for Britain, eh?" he shouted from the winner's rostrum . . . "And for good old football. When's the final?"

"If you're not out in front you don't get on the telly" — *Dutch heat, Enschede 1975*

As anyone who's competed against him will tell you, whether it's on a race-track or at an after-dinner conversation, upstaging Mr James Hunt is rather difficult. "The Shunt" was in good company at Enschede, about an hour and quarter's drive from Amsterdam and almost on the German border.

Emerson Fittipaldi born in Brazil, but for Superstars representing Switzerland through a residential qualification, was still motor racing world champion, Hunt's success yet to come. Holland had Gijs Van Lennep, another driver who'd won Le Mans and the European 5000. There was the handsome blonde giant, also from the host nation of Holland, Ard Schenk, the speed skater who'd won three Olympic gold medals in Sapporo, Japan, and broken records in the process. And, for the first time, a show jumper, the German Hendrik Snoek, no stranger to British Television after his Wembley appearances and his British Derby victory at Hickstead in Sussex.

Hunt, with that public schoolboy charm which has now become one of his trade-marks, was obviously out to enjoy himself but, as we found out, had no intention of letting that get in the way of winning everything he possibly could in every possible way. For the moment however, he was happy to size up the problem.

"Have you seen the thighs on these chaps?" he exclaimed as he saw Schenk and then Sweden's Borje Salming, the ice-hockey player, stripping off. "Blimey, one of their legs is as big as my waist . . . never seen anything like it . . . incredible . . ."

He went muttering on and one has to admit the comparison was noticeable, Hunt tall, lean with that loping walk which tends to make him appear flat-footed — the feet at times looking as if they don't belong to him — and those rounded shoulders which were to be responsible for almost re-writing the weightlifting rule book.

Somebody enquired, quite kindly, if he wished to "get warmed up?" Hunt look at the sky, for once a beautiful blue, and replied: "No thanks, really, I'm quite comfortable. You don't have a large glass of orange juice around by any chance do you? That would be marvellous."

The 100 metres brought Hunt a sixth place. "Delighted," he said "I've started with a success. Old Emerson (Fittipaldi) was seventh, tenth of a second behind me and I intend to beat him at everything." In fact the three racing drivers were 6th, 7th and last. What had happened to the Grand Prix supermen?

15 stone overhead for Malcolm Macdonald in the European final of 1975 . . . and the crowd in the Ahoy Stadium who watched him do it.

I think I must have mentioned it to one of them because straight away, as if they were just playing about, which they certainly weren't, they reversed that completely on the rowing lake. Motor racing 1st (Van Lennep), 2nd (Hunt) and 3rd (Fittipaldi)! But I wasn't the only one a little surprised when I checked the entries for the next event and found that James was in. Weightlifting?

"Well, I've worked all this out you know. I took a look at who was going to have a crack at it and found there was only three — those two guys with the thighs and the footballer (Jeff Jurion, the former Belgian skipper). Now with this O' whatsit formula thing you use, I've got to have some chance because I could be the lightest man," Hunt continued with the expertise. "And in any case, as they give you points down to fifth place, I'm bound to get at least fourth and two points. Right?"

Right, but the way in which he did it wasn't quite as simple. Jurion the footballer, as it turned out just a few pounds lighter than Hunt, elected to have his first lift with the bar weighing 50 kgs (110 lbs). Hunt, full of confidence, or at least trying to con everyone in sight, said: "Is it all right if I don't lift this? I think I'd rather wait until it's a bit heavier. Don't want to use up all my strength too soon you know."

So another 10 kgs was put on. Salming and Schenk, the "guys with the thighs" sat and watched, poker-faced.

"Next lifter, James Hunt Great Britain, 60 kgs."

With a bit of a groan, accompanied by what I can only describe as a look of amazement coupled with sheer terror, he had it half-way, the "clean" position up past the chest and under the chin. Then, with a straight press of the arms, rather than the accepted split of the legs and the jerk, he began to push it upwards.

"Go on, go on," we were all shouting, even the Dutch, the Swedes, Even "the thighs", Messrs Schenk and Salming. There is something about James Hunt that makes you want him to succeed! Hunt pushed. And pushed. The arms were still bent at the elbows, his head almost sticking out of his chest by now. Suddenly he stopped, crashed the weight to the floor and stood there. He looked quite pleased. That is, until the judge said, quite politely, "No lift."

"What?" queried the Surrey-born Wellington College educated Englishman who lives in Spain's jet-set Marbella. "Why not?"

It was explained that the rules of weightlifting say that the arms must be completely straight with the bar held aloft, and held there until the judge signals for it to be put down.

"Really." It was more of a grunt than a reply and he trudged back to the competitors bench, head dropping just a little lower.

Salming, the Swede who'd just signed a million-dollar ice-hockey contract with Toronto Maple Leafs in Canada, and Schenk both decided to have a warm-up lift, tossing the bar up as if it was a match-stick.

Dutch heat (Enschede) 1975
James Hunt "re-writing" the weightlifting
rule book as he proves his arms are
straight—when they're bent!

"Do I have to do everything myself?"
BBC TV producer, Ian Smith, takes our lives
in his hands at Bisley.

It was Hunt's turn again, second attempt. It was a carbon copy of the first, except that he didn't drop the bar. The arms were still bent, the head forward and he stood there, awaiting that judge's signal.

"Well come on then," he spat through clenched teeth as his legs began to totter. "Co . . m . . e   o . . n." And down came the bar. "No lift."

And I think it was at this point that the idea of enjoying it all slipped into the back of Mr Hunt's mind, just a little.

"Look old boy. . . ." He approached the judge and anyone else he could see who appeared, in the remotest way, to resemble authority. "My arms were straight, or as straight as they'll ever be. I'll show you." And he raised his arms overhead, grasping an imaginary 60 kgs, strains — and he's right. The arms of Mr James Hunt are bent when they're straight. If you see what I mean. It was convincing.

"Lift accepted."

"Thank you very much. Christ, what a bloody fuss . . . told 'em that in the first place . . . don't see what all the bother's about . . . of course I'd lifted it. . . ."

And he didn't have to sort it out again. Three unsuccessful attempts at 65 kgs which never reached the "critical point" and Hunt was out, eventually fourth, two points, with Salming lifting 95, Schenk, rather surprisingly, managing only 90.

But this 15¼ stone speed skater one of the legends of the Winter Olympics, was in a class of his own in the cycle race which from previous results was becoming a speed-skater's benefit.

"It's those thighs man. I told you. Look at them." Schenk really was the nearest thing to Garth, the newspaper strip cartoon character and when the programme was transmitted in Britain, a considerable portion of the letters we received afterwards had one general theme. "Picture please . . . address perhaps . . . even telephone number?" Only one went so far as to complain — a letter I received saying I should have more sense (as if *I* ran the BBC) than to put Superstars on television. Rather bemused, I read on to find that the reason for the complaint was that "didn't I realise that it was rather upsetting for ladies on their own to have to watch such great, wonderful hunks of man like that Schenk thing. . . ." P.S. "Is he on again?"

For the record, Hunt was third in the cycle race and very upset by the fact that Fittipaldi was second! The tennis of course was a Hunt benefit and the former junior Wimbledon player sailed through, beating Fittipaldi on the way and losing only one point to his rival. Hendrik Snoek, the German show jumper was quietly collecting points and took the 10 for the shooting and seven more for second place in the swimming. Hunt's football was entertaining (2nd place somehow) while Schnek's was sheer power, five goals out of five, one of them sending Dutch international goalkeeper Piet Schrijvers of Ajax into the back of the net.

But behind the show business, Hunt had kept his promise "to win everything he possibly could in every possible way". Opting out of the torture of the gymn tests ("It's those arms old boy"), he's lying third and only four points away from Salming the leader with just the steeplechase to come. Schenk is between them, Snoek the show jumper fourth.

Hunt at this time was still with Lord Hesketh, the big figure, in more ways than one, who was providing the cars for James to drive, success coming first in the Dutch Grand Prix earlier this same year. And the driver couldn't resist getting the Lord into the act, somehow.

"Ah, yes," he says to me as we record his pre-steeplechase thoughts, "the Lord has promised to turn up here and our plan is for me to get an early lead and then he'll lie down across the track. Nobody is going to get past that obstacle I can tell you!"

In more serious vein, he'd worked out that he had to finish two places ahead of Salming and Schenk, who were beginning to sound like a double-act, to win the heat and qualify for the final. At the gun, he went off as if he was convinced he could do it, taking the first hurdle yards up on the field. We began to believe it as well, just for a moment but then, inevitably, the Hunt pace dropped, and the big two caught up. But the Briton was still hanging on. Snoek the show jumper was just ahead of him but as the German took the water jump, he crashed, plunging into the water in a heap of arms and legs.

As officials rushed to him, the rest went on, Schenk to win, Salming second, Hunt third and third overall, a quite remarkable performance. Schenk the triple gold medallist and Olympic record breaker admits, "That is the hardest thing I have ever done." Salming is, as ever, poker-faced. Hunts asks about Snoek.

By then the German is in a first-aid room having a tetanus injection, leg about to be plastered, arm heavily bandaged. He's spiked himself, ripping his arm open and badly damaging an ankle. I didn't see him again until he came back to show-jumping at Wembley many, many months later. His greeting, though friendly, had a direct reference to the fact that I had convinced him that he would enjoy Superstars!

Hunt had enjoyed it, third placed in this sort of company very impressive indeed. Fittipaldi was last. A few moments before Hunt "took over" the prize giving ceremony, being the expert with giant bottles of champagne, he explained his rather questionable steeplechase tactics, that early energy-sapping burst.

"Ah, dear boy, one thing you learn in motor racing—if you're not out in front at some time or another, you don't get on the telly!"

Belgian heat, Bruges 1975

And then, just for a contrast, there was Ricky Bruch. Bearded and very big—about 20 stone big.

Bruch is the Swedish discus thrower with a bronze medal from the Olympic Games and once world record holder. In Bruges in Belgium you were likely to find him sitting in the corner of the gym "doing his thing", a pair of headphones clapped around his head, the tape recorder at his feet, the deep soul music just now and then producing an occasional twitch through the Bruch frame. In between tapes, he'd produce an electric tooth brush from the hold-all full of potions, pills and elastic strapping—"just a little brush-up on the oral hygiene!"

When it came to the events in the gym, the Swede just sat and watched—until it was his turn. Then, everybody watched. Bruch picked up the weighted medicine ball, a little bigger than a football but looking like a grapefruit in his massive hands. He lies flat on his back, arms outstretched behind him preparing to throw it as he jerks his body upright to a sitting position. Alan Pascoe the British hurdler has reached 10.33 metres with it, Guy Drut the French Olympic medal winning hurdler two metres better.

Bruch inhales a massive breath and then with a roar that echoed around the Rikjssportcentrum—and I'll swear halfway through Bruges—the ball flew from his hands. The judges had marked a number of distance lines on the gym floor but they'd slightly miscalculated. Bruch's ball went past them—and on, and on. The gym wasn't going to be big enough!

With a fat thud like the sound of a heavyweight boxer letting off steam on the heavy punch bag, the ball crashed into the end wall about three feet up. The only way to measure the throw was along the floor to the wall—and then up!

"Check the wall," shouts Pascoe. "I think he's made a hole in it!"

They checked it—and the distance.

"Bruch, Sweden, 19.73 metres."

It was almost twice the distance of all the rest. Drut the Frenchman, full of Gallic charm, couldn't believe it and began to pace out the distance in an exaggerated clown-like style. He looked at the wall where the ball had hit.

"Yeeeach," he shouted. And then burst into peals of laughter, throwing his head back and shaking it in disbelief, his black curly hair emphasising the movement. "Meester Bruch ees Taarzan!"

And no-one disagreed with him—especially when the giant discus thrower picked up a barbell in the weightlifting competition and threw 135 kgs up over his head without raising a grunt or a bead of sweat. Twenty-one and a quarter stone—a Superstars record. Ricky Bruch had made his mark.

(UK National 1976 Aldershot)
The motor racing world champion working on his start.

Great action on the water.

The Barrington affair
Spanish heat at Aldershot 1975

"Welcome to the Spanish heat of The Superstars—and welcome to Aldershot!" Even the start of the whole thing was, to say the least, bizarre.

Britain was staging this next lap as the Spanish delegation had had some little trouble in finding a suitable location, but the change around certainly hadn't affected the quality of the line-up. Jean-Claude Killy, the French ski ace, triple Olympic champion and double world champion was with us after his success in that first ever Superstars in Florida. Tom Okker the Dutch tennis player was also one of the eight and so was the Swede who'd three times broken the world pole-vault record, Kjell Isaksson—a name that was eventually to dominate European Superstars.

For Great Britain it was Jonah Barrington, the great name of squash and a man who prided himself on his fitness and the "peak condition" that he was constantly in.

"Bones" Barrington, the nickname easy to understand once you got a glimpse of the stripped-off frame, had been invited to compete before in one of our own national championships but had been forced to withdraw due to playing commitments. Now he was in, smiling and so obviously looking forward to putting that fitness to the test.

"I don't think I'd better get involved in the speed stuff," he said as he ran his rather wide-staring eyes down the events lists. "And I'm not too keen on the water either, so my opt-outs from the ten will be the 100 metres and the swimming." He gave that little nervous chuckle, running his hand through his dark hair. Neither he nor anyone else could have forecast why he was eventually seen in only half of the compulsory eight events.

Isaksson, the Swede, short for a pole-vaulter, got the 10 points from the 100 metres, Killy second, Barrington watching. It wasn't a terribly fast time (12.1 seconds) and Jonah could well have picked up a few points from the minor placings had he decided to enter. But this former milkman and male model who was rusticated from Trinity, Dublin, before becoming the greatest squash player of his time, was happy to get down to the business of weightlifting.

Only Tom Okker, the tennis player, was sitting this one out; "Not for me, man. I never was the greatest overhead!" After about three-quarters of an hour, it was just Barrington and Isaksson left in, the bar at 80 kgs, just over 176 lbs. The Swede was the heavier man so had to outlift the

(GB heat St. Ives 1976)
Skier Bernard Russi winning the 100 metres at
St. Ives from goalkeeper Peter Shilton.

(UK National 1976 Aldershot)
"Hate the bar" is the weightlifting instruction — and J P R Williams obeys it to the letter.

Briton—and handled the 80 kgs with superb style, full of snap and confidence. We were being given the first real sign of what Isaksson was capable of.

Barrington had already lifted 60, 65, 70 and 75, all at first attempts but as he cleaned the 80 to the half-way position, he appeared for a moment to have just a suspicion of doubt in his mind. And that can be the downfall of a weightlifter, that slight loss of confidence—and Barrington paid for it here in the Fox Gymnasium, unable to straighten his arms as he tried to power it overhead.

"No, no, no," he replied as he was asked if he wanted the second of the three attempts allowed at any one weight. "I'll move on to 85." This meant that he would be allowed only two attempts at this next weight, three successive failures bringing elimination. It was a debatable decision but perhaps he knew his own body better than anyone else. The science of lifting is a gradual build-up of poundage, the psychological barrier of moving up too quickly often too big to overcome.

And coupled with that was the mathematical point—with Isaksson being the heavier man Barrington only had to keep level with him on weight lifted to win. Now, Isaksson was ahead with Barrington doing the chasing to try and catch up.

"Next lifter, Kjell Isaksson, Sweden, 85 kgs on the bar." The officials of the British Amateur Weightlifting Association controlling the contest stand by, a man either end of the bar—the "Spotters"—to take it from the competitor if he is in trouble at any time during the lift.

Isaksson doesn't need them and his style brings a round of applause from the experts as well as the crowd inside the gymnasium.

"Jonah Barrington, Great Britain, same weight 85 kgs, first attempt."

And Barrington now has to try and overcome 10 kgs (about a stone and a half) more than his last successful lift. It is never really on—or up—and he decides he's over-reached himself and retires to take second place to the Swede. Despite the friendly grin across his face as he went through a couple of mock agony gestures, sinking into an untidy heap on the floor, I'm sure the first seeds of what was to follow had been sown.

After he'd won the tennis (easily, bringing just one or two queries from his rivals about allowing the squash man to take part in this) and then just out of the points in the pistol shooting, we were back in the gymnasium, for the last event of the day, the tests. And Barrington was smiling all over his face. This is what he'd really come for, the event that would put the overall fitness of the Superstars under the spotlight. The Barrington banker.

Shock number one—he's fifth out of the seven (Killy the opt-out) in the medicine ball throw and almost three metres down on the winner, Fons Brijdenbach, the young Belgian athlete. But Barrington's not too

(UK National 1976 Aldershot)
"Who got me into this?" David Duckham.

(UK National 1976 Aldershot)
Welsh rugby full back J P R Williams, king of
the dribble.

worried. With those dips and squats to come and with the gym event decided on performances in all three tests, he can make it up.

"Bones", looking good, reaches a count of 25 on the parallel bars before he drops to the ground. That's beaten most, just Brijdenbach and Isaksson to try and match or overtake it. Brijdenbach is finished at 18. Isaksson is on 23, 24. . . . He's using a rather odd "pecking" style, forcing the upper body forward which produces that right angle bend at the elbow but it's legal. Barrington on the bench doesn't move a muscle. Isaksson does 25. He's matched Jonah. And he's beaten him, 26. One more just in case someone had miscounted and Isaksson has the dips, Barrington second and without a word they line up for the squats, a minute of what is generally accepted as "sheer torture" ahead to finish the first day.

Each man has a judge who will count to give his competitor a guide and he'll shout "Not up" if the knees are not brought up to or past the elbows in that front-elevated prone position. The judges are members of the Army School of Physical Training. From the whistle, Tom Okker the tennis player seems to be going the fastest and that's the first surprise. Isaksson is with him but it's Barrington with the higher work rate, more movements to the second than anyone. His judge is shouting, crouching just behind him and now and then tapping the squash player's legs as they pound up and back like a couple of steam pistons. Only Barrington can hear him with the noise of the feet and the shouts of the crowd blotting everything else out.

As the second hand on the chief judge's watch reaches the one minute point and he blows the finish whistle, it looks as if a trip-rope has been pulled around the seven pairs of legs and they collapse into heavy mounds on the platform.

"Scores please," shouts the judge as the Superstars climb slowly to their feet or, in one or two cases, to their knees! Barrington will be the sixth score to be called, Isaksson on the far end will know his result first.

"61 for Isaksson." There's no reaction of any kind from the Swede; Barrington at the other end gives a polite nod of approval. "56 Okker," and that's a tremendous score for this whispy tennis star. "30, 49, 51. . . ." And now Barrington.

As his judge shouts it out, poker-faced, Barrington stiffens. His head whips around to look at the man who's just shouted something that he just simply cannot believe. It's 25, the worst score of all and five less than the portly Spanish golfer Angel Gallardo.

Before anyone can begin to work out the combined points for these three gymnasium tests, Barrington is on his feet. He starts to pound angrily up and down the gymnasium floor as his judge attempts to explain that the knees were simply not coming up to the elbows. So many of the movements were short and couldn't be counted. Suddenly

"Now let's not have any arguments!" James Hunt at Bisley.

The leaders in the 1976 UK National steeplechase with David Duckham about to leap past James Hunt.

ki champion Bernard Russi's 28th dip giving im equal 1st place at St. Ives.

Barrington grabs his track suit top, throws his hold-all across the floor and storms out. The disappointment is clearly too much to take and with the image shattered, he's gone. We wuz, quite definitely, robbed!

The rest of the evening—and a lot of the night—was strange, stories and rumours floating around non-stop as Barrington couldn't be found. Checked out, walked out, in hiding . . . nobody seemed to know. In the early hours of the morning he was found in the hotel but was clearly in no mood to continue his bid for the Superstar title and the second day began without him, despite confirmation from the television play-back that his judge had been right, maybe even generous.

Ironically, Barrington had said only a few minutes before those squat thrusts began: "You're sure this is going to be judged correctly? I've seen some of these so-called squat thrusts before and half of them are never done properly and shouldn't count. I hope the judges have got their eyes open and know what to look for. . . .!"

Isaksson won the two-day heat at the end of it all, a massive 69 points and a new totals record. He'd won six of his eight events outright and then calmly announced that his plan for the final would be "to improve".

Jonah Barrington was invited back into Superstars the following year for the Great Britain Nationals—and was a superb competitor, poking fun at himself and "the black day of my life". In the tennis competition of the 1976 championship, he told us his plan was "to stay on court for the whole of the match and not leave early!" In the gym where the memories came floating back—"I've been looking around for that judge who disqualified me here last time but I can't see him. I think he got sacked from the Army because of it. . . ."

The Barrington smile was back and he finished seventh out of ten but the result, this time, didn't matter. What did matter was that he'd been invited to have another crack at it—and had accepted, prepared to face the publicity his re-appearance would bring. He did well. Unfortunately, the first attempt of this great squash player to become a Superstar is the one that will be remembered.

Spanish heat (Aldershot) 1975
A rare smile from Kjell Isaksson of Sweden as he beats Britain's Jonah Barrington in the dips at Aldershot 1975 and was on his way to setting up the all-time Superstars record points total of 69 in his first appearance in the competition.

The first final—and Hemery goes again
European Final, Rotterdam 1975

Five athletes, two speed skaters, a motor racing driver and a footballer—the nine who, from the forty who'd been competing throughout Europe over the past five weeks, were now together in Rotterdam for this first ever European Superstars Final, the 1975 championship.

There was £11,500 in prize money locked away somewhere and the men who were going to decide it's destiny were a rather distinguished bunch. A world champion: a world record holder and three Olympic gold medals to go with it; two former world record holders, one of them with both gold and bronze Olympic medals; another current world record holder; a record-equalling football goal scorer; and three outstanding national champions.

David Hemery and Malcolm Macdonald were the two British hopes, Hemery getting in as the replacement for Ties Kruize, the Dutch hockey player inuured injured in that car crash. The other nation with two men were the hosts, Holland, and they were relying on two speed skaters, Ard Schenk and Harm Kuipers. Isaksson the pole vaulter was for Sweden; Drut the hurdler for France; little Mariano Haro, the Spanish long distance runner; Fons Brijdenbach, the young Belgian athlete; and Jochen Mass, Germany's Grand Prix driver.

Half of the events were outdoors, half inside the very impressive Ahoy stadium and complex, a massive exhibition and sports centre like Crystal Palace and Olympia rolled into one. Ten thousand spectators, bands, baton twirling girl marchers—it was all there. And so was Supermac Macdonald as they hit the tape on the opening event, the 100 metres. He'd done it again, this time 0.2 seconds faster on the watch than that remarkable 10.9 in Sweden but on this occasion, he'd been one of three given a four metre advantage on handicap, the athletes being allowed to take part and going off scratch.

Inside for cycling, the atmosphere was intense. The banked wooden track and a Dutch crowd who are cycling fanatics. The noise was ridiculous with cow bells and horns clanking and blasting away non-stop. The Dutch crowd had plenty to make a noise about with their two men, the speed-skaters, fighting out the final, Kuipers eventually beating Ard Schenk, the man he was now taking over from in their own sport.

Into the gym. Macdonald heaves the medicine ball to a massive 12.48 metres; Hemery does thirty-seven dips, one more than even Isaksson can manage and then an incredible seventy-eight squat thrusts, again more than Isaksson. But the Swede has it over-all, Hemery's medicine ball throw having been a disaster.

And on it goes, Mass the best swimmer, Schenk the best shot, Isaksson fastest in the rowing boats and Brijdenbach winning the tennis. Schenk again in the football, Isaksson an easy winner at weightlifting. And that just left one event, the 600 metre steeplechase, indoors.

The scoreboard, with nine events gone, told quite a story. Hemery was lying third with 35 points; the big Ard Schenk (with no James Hunt eulogizing over "those thighs, man . . .") was second, a point ahead of Hemery. And top of the table—Isaksson. He's ten points clear and he's got there with a cold, calculated performance that has been planned to the last second and the last centimetre. If he's to be stopped in his tracks now on the way to the title (and winning £5,000 for Swedish athletics, being an amateur) he mustn't be allowed to get a point. And that means five of the seven taking part have got to beat him!

Hemery is walking, by himself, down towards the specially built indoor water jump which isn't far from the finish. "Well, it looks almost as much of a problem as the one in Aldershot," he quips, the memory of his crash in the British heat still very much with him. The best he can hope for is second place but that means £3,000 and Hemery is now a professional. Only Schenk can stop him taking that home to America where he now lives.

It's the handicap again. Isaksson, Kuipers, Macdonald (out of reckoning by now) and Schenk are on the 560 metre mark. Haro the Spaniard is at 585, Hemery and Brijdenbach are scratch, 600 metres to run.

They pass outside the water jump first time as it has to be taken only twice during the race. Haro moves up from fifth to lead and gets a tremendous cheer—he's scored only two points from everything he's done so far. Hemery has caught the pack and already a few are beginning to drop behind but Isaksson is up. Schenk isn't, the pace too hot for the big speed skater and Hemery's chances of that £3,000 are looking very good.

At the water jump for the first time, the leaders, Kuipers, Isaksson, Brijdenbach and Hemery are all over safely. Hemery is running well, and he's going to get the points he needs for that second place and the money. And it looks as if he's going to win the steeplechase for a glory finish.

He rises to the water jump, the last obstacle, with the finish line just ahead. As he hits the thick and solid wooden barrier in front of the water, he crashes through the air sideways, plunging into the water and crunching the left side of his body onto the hard floor beneath. His face is twisted in agony—and Isaksson, then Kuipers leap past him. Hemery somehow scrambles to his feet and half-running, half-falling collapses over the line. As we watch, the ankle is blowing up like a balloon.

Hemery is carried by stretcher to the first-aid room. Typically, as they take him out of the stadium, he glances up at the electronic score-board as it begins to flicker and compute the overall result. He made third place in the steeplechase—and he's got the £3,000 as overall runner-up in the first ever European Superstar Final.

The winner, The Superstar, waits until the last moments to show us that he's human! Seven are on the rostrum in the centre of the Ahoy Sportpaleis, Hemery still in the treatment room with a smashed ankle that is going to put him in plaster, into a wheelchair and then on crutches for six weeks. The lights are dimmed and the voice of the public address announcer echoes around the tiers of seating:

"EUROPEAN SUPERSTAR, KJELL ISAKSSON".

With the fan-fare, Isaksson bursts through the draped curtains at the far end—walking upside down on his hands! The Belgian TV producer, Rik de Saedeleer sums it up. "Zat ees anudder event we will 'ave to forget eef we want to stop 'im winnin' again next year!"

(European final 1976)
Kjell Isaksson, European champion for the
second time.

(UK National 1976 Aldershot)
Jonah Barrington, the reformed Superstar
rebel.

Two of the Magic Moments
UK National, Aldershot 1976

There's not a great deal of similarity between Mr David Starbrook and Mr Stanley Bowles at first sight. One, Mr Starbrook is the "iron man" of judo with a sideboard full of medals including those brought back from the Olympic Games to show for it. Tall, massive hands and a hard, high-cheekboned face that looks as if it has been chiselled out of a rather high-quality granite rock. He doesn't smile a lot.

The other, Mr Bowles, is smaller. A lot smaller. He has longer hair and a body that many football defenders claim this England international can thread through the eye of a needle. He hates flying, not too keen on water either and has a passionate love of horses and greyhounds, when they're running professionally. "I used to have a greyhound bitch but sold her when I found I could run faster than she could!"

As I say, not exactly twin brothers Mr Starbrook and Mr Bowles, but it was these two who produced two moments in the 1976 British Superstars championship that were sheer magic.

There are ten top British sportsmen, once again at Aldershot, Hemery, Conteh, Hunt, Macdonald and Barrington among them. The newcomers to the scene, together with Bowles and Starbrook, are the rugby players David Duckham, J.P.R. Williams and Gareth Edwards. The two footballers, Mac and Stanley, went a long way to proving what that newspaper TV critic had said: "They're putting the fun back into sport." It mightn't have been all that funny to them, at the time, but their capsizes in the same heat of the canoeing (the new event taking over from rowing) brought the safety boat and the frogmen racing into action. Both lived to boast about it—or deny it—with Conteh having given a graphic description of how *he* nearly drowned when he was practising in a canal. The 1974 British Superstar had apparently overturned and was half-trapped underneath.

"I'm telling ya, straight up, I'm waving me arms about like mad and this dear old lady is the only blinkin' person in sight. So I shout and wave a bit more—and do ya know what she does? Bleedin' waves back and walks off, tha's right, 'onest."

He's learned a bit though and is second to Hemery, Hunt third, Starbrook fourth.

Gareth Edwards lifts a bar weighing exactly 100 kgs to beat the rest out of sight. Hemery has the cycling from Hunt, Williams the tennis from Barrington (who's beaten Hunt on the way to upset the form book completely). And we have come to Bisley for the pistol shooting.

(*UK National 1976 Aldershot*)
Footballers and canoes just don't seem to mix! Mr. Macdonald and Mr. Bowles on their way to the rescue boat, UK National, 1976.

Hemery, Conteh and Duckham have all shot the same score with a .38 calibre pistol, 46 out of 50. The fourth man to approach the firing point is Bowles. The judge's voice booms out: "Aim and shoot."

Bowles has been watching his rivals, all of them now sitting in a multi-coloured, track-suited line on a bench behind him, the estimated safe distance from the marksman. He raises his arm, very straight, takes aim and squeezes the trigger. The shot slams into the target fifteen metres away and a puff of sand spurts up behind. Bowles, very correctly, lowers the straight arm to the table, the pistol in line, and rests the tip of the barrel on the green baize cloth.

At which point, nine superstars, the range officer and just about everybody else at Bisley leap for cover.

The crack of another shot had echoed around the range. Bowles stiffened as his arm jerked — and looked in horror at the table. A hole glared back at him!

Stanley, obviously pleased at getting the first shot away very professionally had, in his excitement or relief, flexed his finger muscles with alarming results. The shot must have missed his foot half under the table by very little and he went a distinctive shade of grey-white. As his rivals clambered to their feet, realising that Bowles had not decided to eliminate them from the competition in a rather unorthodox manner, they began to tell and show each other exactly what had happened. Fingers were pointing, arms outstretched and it was Starbrook who just couldn't believe it all.

The big judo man broke into great roars of near-hysterical laughter, holding his hands to his head and rocking to and fro on the bench. Bowles, after some talk about "a pistol malfunction" was allowed to continue, rather less people near him than before! But no-one could recover from that and the footballer was last with 20 scored. Hunt incidentally tied with the three leaders on 46, with Hemery winning the shoot-off, four bulls and a nine, from Conteh. But it was Stanley's event, in the same way that one later that day in the gymnasium was Starbrook's.

The medicine ball throw had now been dropped, just the dips and the squats to worry about — and that's still enough for anyone. Dips first and the scores begin to pile up. John Conteh, who'd shared the tests with Hemery when they met in 1974, is finished at 30; Hemery a magnificent 38 and that has surely got it sewn up; Macdonald ("I hate this") 17; Gareth Edwards, looking just a little weighty around the middle, 27; J.P.R. Williams, his Welsh colleague and the greatest rugby full back in the world, is shattered at 12. Then Duckham, 27, the same as Edwards and more than he'd expected; Barrington, laughing about it all now, 21. Just David Starbrook left to try and get near Hemery and the big man wraps his massive hands around the parallel bars. His feet aren't too far off the ground as he drops for the first time but it's all right, he's not touching, the height of the bars having been correctly adjusted.

Starbrook, impassive, is pumping well, 15, 16, 17, 18. He's past the score of Williams and Macdonald. . . .28, 29, 30, 31 . . . Conteh's score beaten and only Hemery is above that with 38. Hemery more than anyone else can't take his eyes off the almost poker-like Starbrook frame, shoulders bunched as he drops and then the muscles in his upper arms pushing them back up again.

The judge is shouting the score. "Thirty-five . . ." Starbrook is slowing down. "Thirty-six . . . thirty-seven. . . ." He's almost stopped . . . "Thirty-eight!" Level with Hemery—and Starbrook is motionless as he's pushed himself upright again, arms locked straight. He looks straight ahead, and then to his left and right. You can hear a pin drop and you can hear Hemery breathing—just!

Starbrook catches Hemery's staring eyes—and with the most outrageous wink I've ever seen, begins to pump his arms up and down faster than he's been doing from the start: 39, 40, 41, 42. . . . The judge can hardly keep up and Hemery's mouth drops open in amazement.

Within a second or two, Starbrook decides he's made the point and drops down. The judge, amid the applause and a fair amount of laughter, shouts "Forty-nine," and Starbrook stops in his tracks. "Really? I only stopped because I thought I'd reached 50. Ah well, never mind, bit o' fun wasn't it?"

Indeed it was. He does seventy-four squats to Hemery's seventy-six and they share the gym event, Conteh third and a very impressive 4th place for David Duckham, the England rugby three-quarter. Duckham also took the steeplechase from James Hunt (another fast start) with Hemery and Starbrook opting out. The points added up to a Hemery win, 49½ to Conteh's 29 and the athlete had got his revenge over the man who'd taken the Superstar title off him in 1974. For the record, Starbrook was 6th, Bowles last but unanimously first and second in the entertainment stakes.

Kevin Keegan — and others — *European Series: British heat, St. Ives, Dutch heat, Vlaardingen; Belgian heat, Bracknell 1976*

John Conteh doesn't take defeat lightly and when we met up again in June, this time at St. Ives in Huntingdonshire, for the start of the new European run of Supersars, he was just a little disappointed that Hemery wasn't there as well. His old rival was to take part in a later heat on the way to "Superstar of Europe 1976" and Conteh was saying "I've never felt better."

He was very much in the mood for a fight, having suffered the frustrations of the broken hand, postponements of the projected world title defence against Alvaro Lopez and then more hand trouble during training. Plans were already under way, with the hand repaired, for a meeting with Lopez in Copenhagen (which Conteh eventually won in October) and he was "Rarin' to go, man!" Peter Shilton, the England football goalkeeper, was the second Great Britain competitor in this home heat with a collection of winter sports stars (including Bernard Russi, Switzerland's Olympic gold and silver medallist) and Maurice Maertens, the Belgian World Cup footballer.

The skiers and the skaters were of the same breed as the motor racing drivers — hard and very competitive. Shilton, after a good second place to Russi in the 100 metres, found it hard going and Conteh was having to work even harder than he did against Hemery to stay with it. But helped by a gigantic eighty squat thrusts in the gym, he made it, qualifying for Europe with that now famous quote "This is no longer a joke . . ." and picked up another first prize, this time 5,000 dollars, 10,000 being the prize ahead for the final.

David Wilkie came to Vlaardingen in Holland for the next one and he was there, straight out of the water of Montreal and still carrying his swimming gold medal everywhere he went. And who could blame him.

He had some good results, including an outright victory in the football event, beating Holland's international goal keeper Piet Schrijvers of Ajax three times out of three in the slalom/dribbling test and then twice in five attempts from the penalty spot. It had to be the biggest Scottish bonus of all time! But during the second day, he faded after a gallant second in the gymnasium where we were appreciating the actions of our first-ever ski-jumper Superstar.

This was Karl Schnabl, the young Austrian Olympic champion, the man who in Innsbruck launched himself from the top of a man-made shute about the same height as St. Paul's Cathedral and then, at over seventy miles an hour, sailed through the air on skis for roughly the same

British heat (St. Ives) 1976.
"You don't catch me doing this one . . . . !"
John Conteh opts out of the cycling in the
British heat at St. Ives, but goes on to win the
title and qualify for the European final.

distance as Wembley's football pitch, goal-mouth to goal-mouth. When he hit the ice and snow, still travelling at about the same speed, he'd won the Olympic gold medal in front of his own crowd in one of the most spectular sports you'll ever see.

Now he was showing us that there was a lot more to him than just that (*Just* that?) and finished a clear winner, nine points ahead of the Swedish speedway rider, Anders Michanek, who's spent so much of his time with English clubs. Walter Spanghero, the giant French rugby forward, had to take last place of the eight with thirteen points. He attempted to explain to us that thirteen didn't matter; he wasn't superstitious. In fact he didn't worry about very much — Big Walter was on his honeymoon! Last in the 100 metres, last in the swimming, the squat thrusts a nightmare. . . .

And so to Kevin Keegan. It's the Belgian heat at Bracknell in Berkshire, another of those "Spanish heat in Aldershot" situations with Britain able to provide the venue that Belgium couldn't arrange at that very moment. It's very hot, the end of June, the programme to be seen on television in December.

Although the greatest downhill ski champion of all time, Franz Klammer, had been flown in from Austria and Rudi Krol the Dutch international footballer was there as well, the little England and Liverpool player was, by the end of the two days, the only man everyone was talking about. And I for one will be talking about Keegan and his Superstar performance for a long time yet.

100 metres (Opt-out, unhappy about an old leg injury)

Football (Banned)

Canoeing (Win)

Weightlifting (Win)

Table tennis (Runner-up)

Swimming (3rd)

Shooting (3rd)

Gym tests (4th)

Cycling . . . and this is where Kevin Keegan was responsible for at first, the most frightening moment of Superstars and then two of the most courageous.

The bike race was over a distance of 470 metres, two men per heat which were time trials, the fastest men overall later riding off for 1st and 2nd place.

Heat 1 and Klammer logs a time of 43.2 with Rudi Krol, the Dutch footballer, breaking down and granted a re-ride later.

Heat 2 and it's Jean-Pierre Coopman, the Belgian heavyweight boxer (47.2) beating Stellan Bengtsson, the Swedish world table tennis champion.

Heat 3 and it's Keegan on the inside start position, drawn against

(UK National 1976 Aldershot)
The shock of the tennis, Hunt the junior Wimbledon player beaten by Barrington in the semi-finals at Aldershot.

The Iron Man of Judo, Dave Starbrook in trouble—with the iron! (UK National 1976 Aldershot).

Gilbert Van Binst, the Belgian and Anderlecht football captain. The gun — and they're away together but Van Binst is looking happer than Keegan. The Liverpool player is pushing with every muscle he's got on his pedals and suddenly wobbles a little half-way up the starting straight with the first bend in sight. He corrects it, beginning to look a little happier now as Van Binst prepares to take the first corner just less than bike length up on Keegan. As they go into it, Van Binst leading to the left, Keegan's front wheel touches the back wheel of the Belgian's machine.

Keegan's back wheel skids off to the right towards the inside of the track, the front wheel whips back on itself and Keegan is catapulted off as if he's been shot out of a cannon.

He's wearing a cycling crash helmet but it's his right shoulder and then his elbow which hit the bone-dry, dusty, cinder track here at the Bracknell stadium. And hit it hard. He skids, head first across the lanes, almost buried in a cloud of dust and cinder particles, his back now carrying the rest of his body along like a snow-sled. Finally after what seems like an age, he lies still, the dust now about three feet high above him.

It's all taken about three seconds.

In that three seconds, people inside the track on the grass field have started to run, with Ken Hawkes of the T.W.I. promoting company with them, but pleading, if you can plead at the top of your voice; "GET OFF THE TRACK, GET OFF THE TRACK, KEEP AWAY FROM HIM . . . Christ. . . ."

Meanwhile, Van Binst has pulled up, looking back to see what has happened. By now, Keegan, still lying there, is surrounded by just about everyone who could reach the track and there's a uniformed medical attendant on his way over, his bag banging against his waist.

Keegan sits up, not quite sure where he is and slowly gets to his feet. There's a lump of skin missing from his elbow about the size of a small beer mat but it's his back which brings the intakes of breath from those of us crowded around him. The whole of one shoulder and half-way down the back, where the singlet he was wearing has been scraped away, is a red and black mass of cuts and dirt.

"It's O.K., it's O.K." he keeps insisting. "I'm all right, don't worry about it. Not half as bad as you get in football . . . honest, I'm O.K." It's just as well he's the only person in the stadium who can't see his back.

He comes with us into the first-aid room refusing to go to hospital and confirming that he's had a tetanus injection only recently. He's cleaned up and then comes with me back out into the centre. "I think I ought to let them see I'm O.K." he says. The cheer when he appears is deafening and as I interview him, he takes any possible blame away from Van Binst and then as I wish him luck and speedy recovery, he calmly announces:

(UK National 1976 Aldershot)
Supermac Macdonald, always the fastest.

Edwards and Conteh in flight during the UK National steeplechase.

David Hemery in training for the bike race.

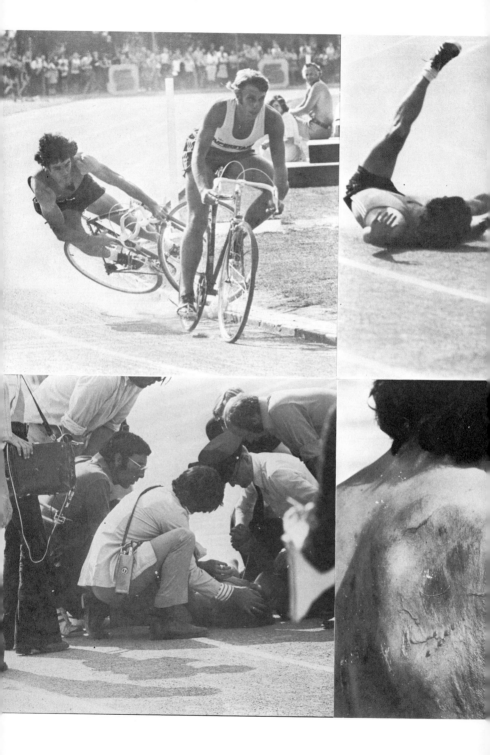

The most terrifying and most courageous moments in Superstars. England footballer Kevin Keegan at Bracknell, 1976.

"Oh, I'm not going home yet. I'd like to have another go if they'll let me—I'm all right."

He has another go, arm bandaged and obviously finding it very uncomfortable to sit on a bicycle saddle crouched over a pair of racing handlebars. Van Binst has also been given another ride to get a qualifying time, being paired with Krol, the other mechanical failure. So Keegan is on his own.

Somehow he puts up the second fastest time of all which means he can face Klammer, the fastest, in the match-race final. Ignoring those of us who suggest he should settle for the second place he's already got—"No David, these people here in the stands have come here to see me make a fool of me'self and they've got a right to it. . . ." Keegan rides again, yet another lap and a half of the track and is just beaten by the downhill skier.

Half an hour later, Keegan is round the track again, this time 600 metres in the steeplechase, leaping hurdles and water jumps. And wins it. As he crosses the line I run towards him with a microphone. He collapses over my arm signalling that he can't speak and grasps a cardboard cup of water someone hands him like it was champagne. "Never again, never again," he gasps.

And he didn't do it again, footballing commitments genuinely keeping him out of the final he'd qualified for as the Superstar in this heat. When I saw him quite a long time afterwards and we talked about it he said: "I think that took a few years off me—but I wouldn't mind another crack . . . sometime. . . .".

I hope I'm there.

The last two laps—and the '76 final
French heat, Vichy; European Final, Rotterdam 1976

"Stay cool, man—stay cool". Marcello Fiasconaro was the speaker, the part-English, part-South African, part-Italian who used to play rugby, turned athelete, broke the world 800 metre record and is now going back to rugby. Marcello was talking to David Hemery who was finding the tension of a re-match with Kjell Isaksson here on the Swede's home ground rather more of a mental than a physical problem.

The 1975 winner and runner-up, Isaksson and Hemery were in a heat together with Fiasconaro which everyone agreed should have been the final, certainly in terms of the strength of the line-up. Frank Nusse was in, Holland's top hurdler and their own national superstar title-holder; and so was Sten Stensen the Norwegian who won a gold at speed skating in the Olympic Games. And there was Johan Granath, another Swedish speed skater, a double world champion, a very big and powerful man. François Mathy, the Olympic bronze medal show jumper from Belgium and Daniel Morelon of France who's won almost every thing invented in cycling, made up the weight—and the eight.

And Hemery was anything but "cool". Isaksson was, as ever, detached from it all. While the rest sit and watch the pistol shooting, he shuts his eyes with his hand clad in thick gloves—"the fingers you see, they must not get cold. My coach told me about this. . . ." For a lot of the time, he's on his own, just a word now and then with his fellow-countryman Granath and the occasional remark to Hemery. But it's hardly a conversation.

The four athletes are 1, 2, 3 and 4 in the sprint, Hemery the best. Isaksson shoots, canoes, plays table tennis, and runs the steeplechase, every time better than anyone else. The luck, if there is any around, is certainly not flying Hemery's way, even getting involved in a protest in the gym tests where he beats the Swede on the dips but is down in the squats, at first being awarded only sixty-four. Referee Mike Campbell-Lamerton, the former British Rugby Lion who is the touring, resident official goes into conference and emerges with the decision. Hemery is upgraded to seventy-six but that's only 3rd best.

"British justice prevails," Hemery half-laughs—but it is only half a laugh because he knows that makes him second—and Isaksson has won the gym event as well!

But again, it's the cycling where Hemery continues his Superstar trail of misfortune following those crashes at water jumps in previous steeplechases. Like Keegan, Hemery has another spectacular fall and at first I thought he'd landed on his face. He escapes with just a scraped thigh on a wet, tartan track and re-rides. But his luck, or lack of it, has him paired with a speed-skater in the final he qualifies for, and the speed-skater is a world champion, Granath.

That doesn't stop the British hurdler and now almost professional Superstar on both sides of the Atlantic attacking Granath in the ride for first and second place. He almost comes off in exactly the same spot but rides out of trouble and into second place. Isaksson hadn't entered.

And that meant Hemery hadn't made the Superstars final, third place overall and 36.33 points (Granath second to the inevitable Isaksson)—not good enough.

That was decided a couple of weeks later in Vichy in France where Gareth Edwards despite coming fourth, scored more points (42.5) and pushed Hemery out; Edwards and Conteh our top men from the heats. The French heat in Vichy was glorious for one reason—the completely unexpected triumph of the Wimbledon tennis champion Bjorn Borg who won it in style, stood on the winner's rostrum after two days in which the rain had never stopped ("I've heard of Vichy water but this is ridiculous," said Edwards from somewhere under an umbrella) and the significance of Borg's win became very apparent indeed.

On one side of him in second place was France's Guy Drut who'd won the gold medal in the Montreal Olympics at 110 metre hurdles. On the other side, the bearded Ivo Van Damme of Belgium, two silver medals from the same Games, 800 and 1500 metres (Van Damme later tragically and fatally injured in car accident, December 29th 1976). Borg had beaten both of them but ironically, so sure he wouldn't come anywhere near a win, had already booked himself for a tennis tour and like Keegan was out of the final.

A week later, eleven were in, the top eleven available from the five heats and forty champion sportsmen, fourteen of whom had won medals in Olympic Games. Back to the Ahoy in Rotterdam, where there was a 10,000 dollars first prize, another 13,000 dollars for the places. And the performances of the eleven lived up to a final and that sort of money.

There were disappointments—the biggest for us was that Gareth Edwards, after the soaking in Vichy, had caught 'flu and was in and out of bed like a yo-yo, and a rather sick one. He managed only four of the eight events he was supposed to do but still lifted 100 kgs in the weightlifting—in this sort of company good enough for only fourth place.

Johan Granath was the giant and as he raised the final bar over his head, it visibly sagged at each end. There were 115 kgs on it, over 18 stone and even then he didn't beat Isaksson. The defending European champion had somehow snapped up 105 and being almost three stones lighter on body weight, he was yet again, a winner.

Edwards produced the remark of the final after he climbed, once again, out of his bed a few moments after the rest had completed gym tests. We told him that Karl Schnabl the ski-jumper had beaten every record in the book, even Dave Starbrook's, with fifty-three dips, calmly annoucing in broken English to the amazed on-lookers as he reached the half century; "This . . . this 'ees 'ard wurk!"

"Good God," said Edwards when we told him. "If I'd seen that I'd have had a heart-attack rather than just the 'flu!"

Another record went in the cycling, the massive Granath powering around the banked track in a pursuit race with Schnabl in the final, and despite the Austrian ski-jumper almost causing a pile-up on the last bend. The speed-skater's time for the four laps and 800 metres was exactly one minute. That was faster than some professional cyclists who'd been racing there a few days before.

John Conteh never got a look in. He'd defended his world boxing title, was too relaxed and lacked the fire and drive of his previous performances. And it was Granath who took the last set of 10 points in the steeplechase, Isaksson content to finish second and keep out Schnabl, the only man who by now had a chance of upsetting a Swedish double. Schnabl shared the second place with Granath and Frank Nusse, the Dutch athlete was fourth.

So Isaksson had kept his European Superstar title and with the top four men all amateurs, the pot of gold (or dollars) all went to the benefit of the sports they represent. I think I probably echoed the thoughts of most people when, at the end of our BBC programme over the Christmas Holiday, with Isaksson again "The Superstar", I said "Just where do you find a man to beat him."

To do that, or at least to try, we had to go a few thousand miles or so across the Atlantic Ocean to America's deep south and the first ever World Superstars Championship.

Georgia — on everyone's mind!
World Superstars championship

"Man, ah bin here four days 'n ah ent sin a cotton field yit!"

Liverpudlian come southerner, Mr John Conteh, fresh from his successful world boxing title defence against American Len Hutchins was camping it up with the World Superstars in the Callaway Gardens restaurant, Pine Mountain, Georgia, U.S.A.

There were fifteen Superstars with us in this typically American huntin', fishin' and shootin' country club, a few hours drive from Florida where The Superstars had first started way back in 1973. Then it was an unknown, untried experiment. Now countries all over the world were either staging their own Superstar championship or planning to. And fifteen men — world champions, world record holders, Olympic medal winners and Superstar champions — had been jetted in to Pine Mountain for what was being called "WORLD SUPERSTARS I".

Conteh and the Welsh rugby genius Gareth Edwards were here for Great Britain; Edwards worried about getting back for his 49th rugby international, Wales v Scotland at Murrayfield where a victory would give Wales the Triple Crown. "If I don't make it by Friday for training in Cardiff, they'll throw me out — and I'm talking about the country not just the team — honest, I'm not joking. I've got to get back even if it means chartering Concorde from the front lawn here to my back garden!"

The jokes were coming from everyone, Conteh in particular, the pre-championship nerves and apprehension intensified by the thoughts of that prize-money. It was going to be possible to win 70 points over the two days with 300 US dollars for every single one. And if that wasn't enough, there was a 25,000 US dollar bonus for the winner, 15,000 for runner-up, 10,000 for third . . . and on it went. A total of 132,000 dollars in the prize money bucket.

The fifteen had come from nine nations and seven sports; nine Olympic medals between them with the number of world records held or broken just about countless. The Americans were relying on professional footballers and Bob Seagren, the pole-vaulter who'd won that first ever Superstars in Rotunda. He'd twice been runner-up since then, and another pole-vaulter knew how he'd won every point. The other vaulter was, of course, Kjell Isaksson, unbeaten in Europe and, as usual, telling everyone here that he was "tired . . . haven't been able to train like the Americans . . . don't stand much of a chance. . . ."

No-one believed a word of it.

The temperature was in the high 80s and the asphalt track which had been laid in five weeks was baking to the touch as the 100 yards was set up. Edwards wasn't fast enough in the second heat either and the final saw another American footballer, Billy "White Shoes" Johnson winning it in 9.9 seconds.

We couldn't help wondering what Malcolm Macdonald would have done against that, remembering his 100 metres times in Europe.

The full implication of the prize money structure was beginning to sink in and it really hit everyone when the football competition took place — or "this damned British soccer business" as the Americans insisted in calling it.

It was just five shots at a goalkeeper, an ex-Crystal Palace player, Paul Hammond, now with Tampa Bay Rowdies. Conteh put four of the five past him but so did four others including, to our horror, two American footballers. Edwards was the last to go, knowing that a maximum five goals would mean a win and 3,000 dollars.

Goal, Goal, Goal, Goal — and Edwards turned to glance at us on the side-line. One more and he'd got it and I swear that as he turned back to face the goal, it looked to him like a giant cash register with a 3,000 dollar sign waiting there for him to ring up. He hit the ball, and the 'keeper pulled off one of his best saves of the day. Edwards has missed it — and in the six man kick-off for first place it was Guy Drut the winner, Edwards. Conteh and four others equal second; 840 dollars instead of 3,000. One kick had cost the Welshman almost £1,300.

The weightlifting bore little resemblance to the competitions that had brought so much tension to the British and European Superstars. The bar was already on a chest high stand and had only to be jerked overhead for a lift, man against man regardless of body weight. However, it was remarkable for one reason. Isaksson, the smallest, beating everyone except the 16¼ stone American Dave Casper; the Swede hoisting almost 19 stone overhead!

Already, any hopes of a British success had gone. Edwards was having muscle trouble again, back, leg and elbow, that rugby international match very much in his mind. Conteh was still laughing and joking despite putting every ounce of effort into each one of his seven events, but the class was telling. So was the temperature, and at the end of the cycle race where a lap marker's error made the finalists ride a "five-lap four-lap event", Bob Seagren collapsed and it took five minutes or so and an oxygen cylinder to bring him round.

Despite that, he ran an incredible race in the new event, the commando-type obstacle race, 12 feet high walls, tackle dummies, water jumps and all. His second place was enough — and Seagren, the first Superstar, was the first world champion, 37,000 dollars richer.

At the end of it all, sipping Coke — we were in a "dry county" believe it

73

The Keegan brand of determination — and one can't help wondering what result it might have brought had he been one of Great Britain's competitors in the World Superstars Championship!

or not—we thought about the people who'd said, when the Superstar idea was first made public, *"IT'LL NEVER WORK".*

And yet in four years:

An American footballer, Kyle Rote Jnr who wasn't even in the world final has won over £100,000 from it.

New Zealand's triple gold medal athlete Peter Snell has financed his educational career from it.

A new profession has been established: "Professional Superstar".

The world's most successful sportsmen are queueing up to take part.

And the countless millions who watch it have made it the most successful sports series on television.

Dick Button, the American who launched it, says: "We haven't really started yet. This is just the overture."

My thoughts? There's room for changes, improvements (where isn't there?), perhaps a re-think on the money side of it; with the vast sums involved it's capable of doing more than just providing an even bigger prize fund. But it's brought a new dimension to sport, tapped undiscovered talent and re-introduced the fun and enjoyment into world class competition.

IT'S WORKED

Biographies

AGOSTINI, Giacomo (Italy). Motor cycling. Born June 16, 1942. Lives in Bergamo. Joined MV—Agusta works team 1965, Japan's Yamaha team 1974, rejoined MV year later and also races his own Suzuki-4. Eight times 500 cc world champion, seven times 350 cc. Five times Senior TT champion Isle of Man. From 1965 to mid-1976 had record 121 world championship wins including a record nineteen in 1970. Film-star "pin-up" in three feature films.
Superstars record: Sweden, 1975 (6th, 20 points). Best performance: 1st, rowing.

ARCARI, Bruno (Italy). Boxing. Born Frosinone on New Year's Day, 1942. Amateur boxer from age of fifteen. International and world military champion 1963 and 1964. Tokyo Olympic Games (lightweight) 1964, retired hurt versus Oundo of Kenya. Professional later 1964, won World Junior Welterweight title and made nine successful defences between 1970 and 1974. European Junior Welterweight champion 1968, world champion 1970.
Superstars record: French heat, 1976 (7th, 10 points).
Best performances: 3rd, weightlifting and swimming.

BARRINGTON, Jonah (G.B.) Squash. Born Cornwall 1941, father Irish. Ex-milkman and male model, rusticated after two years at Trinity College, Dublin. British Amateur champion 1966, 1967, 1968. British Open champion (acknowledged world championship) 6 times 1966-72. Fitness fanatic, nicknamed 'Bones'.
Superstars record: Spanish heat (Aldershot), 1975. Walked out after first day following dispute over squat thrust score. U.K. National, Aldershot, 1976 (7th out of 10, 18 points).
Best performance: 1st, tennis 1975.

BELL, Colin (G.B.). Football. Born Hesleden, 1948. England international, Bury and Manchester City. At end of 1975-76 season had made over 400 League appearances for two clubs and scored 140 goals. Described by Malcolm Allison as "Nijinsky". First England caps 1968 v Sweden and West Germany. Total to June 1976, 48.
Superstars record: UK National (Crystal Palace), 1974 (3rd, 41 points). British heat (Aldershot), 1975 (3rd, 37 points).
Best performances: 1st, shooting and steeplechase, 1974. 1st steeplechase, 1975.

BELL, OLIN "Corky" (Belgium). Basketball. Born New York City, July 12, 1946. All-state graded player at high school. All-American in Chicago where he majored in mathematics and physical education. Moved to Belgium 1968, Belgian citizen 1973. Belgian international attached to Belgian Air Force. Stands 6'3" tall, likes gardening, soul music and cars.
Superstars record: Dutch heat (Holland), 1976 (equal 3rd, 32 points). Euro final (Holland), 1976. (8th out of 11, 14 points).
Best performances: 2nd, weightligting, 100 metres and steeplechase (heat) equal 2nd, soccer skills (final).

BENGTSSON, Stellan (Sweden). Table Tennis. Twenty-four years old. International over 100 times. Won three world titles (Singles 1971, Doubles and Team 1973). European champion Singles 1972, Doubles 1976 and Team 1968, 1970, 1972 and 1974. Twelve Swedish titles. Lives at Falkenberg. 12-handicap golfer.
Superstars record: Belgian heat (Bracknell), 1976 (6th, 15 points).
Best performance: 2nd, soccer skills.

BJERRE, Kresten (Denmark). Football. Aged thirty-one. 23 caps, based in Netherlands for past seven years. Played for PSV Eindhoven and then moved to Racing White Daring Molenbeek in Belgium. Played more League games in Belgium than any other player—over 200. Lives at Wezembeek-Oppem. Keen tennis player.
Superstars record: Dutch heat (Holland), 1976 (5th, 29 points).
Best performance: 1st, steeplechase.

BLYTH, Charles "Chay" (G.B.). Sailing. Born 1940, Hawick, Scotland. Ex-paratrooper. 1966 rowed across Atlantic with Captain John Ridgeway. 1968 sailed around world in "British Steel" East to West. 1973-74 sailed West to East in Great Britain II. Lecturer. Awarded CBE and BEM.
Superstars record: UK National (Crystal Palace), 1974 (6th out of 7, 22.50 points).
Best performance: 1st, rowing.

BORG, Bjorn (Sweden). Lawn tennis. Born June 6, 1956 on a Swedish National Holdiay 40 km from Stockholm. Began playing tennis when nine after father had given him a racquet he had won in a table-tennis tournament. Taught by Percy Rosberg and Lennart Bergelin and made Davis Cup debut when fifteen (beat Onny Parun of New Zealand). Reached 5th round Wimbledon on first appearance 1973. Won French and Italian championships and US Pro title 1974. Retained French and US Pro and won Spanish 1975, winning 220,000 dollars. Won Wimbledon beating Nastase 1976, and WCT Singles, Dallas. 1976 earnings: over 400,000 dollars.
Superstars record: French heat (Vichy), 1976 (champion, 55 points). Unable to accept place in final due to tennis tour.
Best performances: 1st table-tennis, canoeing, football penalties, steeplechase.

BOUTTIER, Jean-Claude (France). Boxing. Born Vitry, October 13, 1943. 5' 9¾'' tall. Won European Middleweight title June 1971 beating Juan Carlos Duran in Paris, on points, 15 rounds. Retained title when he knocked out Bunny Sterling of G.B. six months later in 14th round, also in Paris. Stripped of title for failing to defend, won it back in March 1974 and lost it to Kevin Finnegan (G.B.), April 1974 on points.
Superstars record: British heat (Aldershot), 1975 (8th, 1½ points).
Best performance: equal 4th, football penalties.

BOWLES, Stanley (G.B.). Football. Born in Manchester, twenty-seven years old. England international, first cap 1974 versus Portugal. Six seasons with Manchester City, then Bury, Crewe Alexandra, Carlisle, Q.P.R. Over 250 league appearances, Hates flying. Horse and greyhound racing fan (ex-owner). Controversial temperament.
Superstars record: UK National (Aldershot), 1976 (10th out of 10, 7 points).
Best performance: 3rd, swimming.

BRIJDENBACH, Alfons "Fons" (Belgium). Athletics. Born October 12, 1954. 6' 1''. European Junior 400 metre champion 1973, European Indoor champion 1974. In the Olympic Games in Montreal 1976 clocked a personal best time of 45.04 seconds for 4th place, the best European. Lives at Peer. P.E. student.
Superstars record: Spanish heat (Aldershot), 1975 (2nd, 41 points. European final Rotterdam), 1975 (5th, 21 points).
Best performances: 1st, soccer skills (heat). 1st, tennis (final).

BRUCH, Ricky (Sweden). Athletics. Born July 2nd, 1946. 6' 6¼'' tall, 20 stone 2 lbs. World discus record holder 1972 (68.40 metres) and won event in Europa Cup final 1970. Bronze medallist Olympic Games in Munich, 8th in Mexico, didn't qualify

Montreal. Silver medal European championships in Athens 1969 and bronze in Rome.
Superstars record: Belgian heat (Bruges), 1975 (5th, 33.5 points).
Best performance: 1st, weightlifting (135 kgs).

BUGNER, Joe (G.B.). Boxing. Born March 13, 1950 in Hungary. Naturalised Briton 1967. 6′ 4″ weighs around 15 stone 10 lbs. Youngest ever boxer to win all three Heavyweight titles, British, Empire and European. Controversial win over Henry Cooper on March 16th 1971. Fought Muhammad Ali and Joe Frazier, losing to both. Ex-discus thrower. Retired from boxing and then recently made a come-back to beat Richard Dunn and win back three titles.
Superstars record: UK National (Crystal Palace), 1973 (equal 3rd, 25 points).
Best performances: 1st, shooting and weightlifting.

CHANNON,   Mike (G.B.). Football. Born Orcheston, Wilts. 6′ 0½″, weight around 12 stone, size 7½ shoe. England international and Southampton. First cap 1973 versus Yugoslavia, thirty-five England appearances to June 1976. Scored five goals during FA Cup winning run by Southampton 1976; leading goal scorer in Divison 1 1973-74 season. At end of 1975-76 season had scored 138 goals and made over 350 league appearances. Breeds horses.
Superstars record: UK National (Crystal Palace), 1974 (7th out of 7, 21 points).
Best performance: 1st, 100 metres.

CONTEH,   John (G.B.). Boxing. Born May 27, 1951, Liverpool. Amateur boxing from age of ten and won gold medal in Commonwealth Games 1970. Moved to London and in 1973 won British and Commonwealth Light-Heavyweight Pro title from Chris Finnegan, European title from Rudi Schmidtke (W. Ger.) and then world title, beating Jorge Ahumada (Arg.) in 1974. Retained world crown versus Alvaro Lopez (U.S.)., Copenhagen, October 9, 1976. Retained world title again versus Len Hutchins (U.S.), Liverpool, March 5, 1977. Had trouble with right hand, twice breaking it.
Superstars record: UK National (Crystal Palace), 1974 (champion, 57.83 points). UK
                     National (Aldershot), 1976 (runner-up, 29 points). British heat
                     (St. Ives), 1976 (champion, 42.5 points). European final
                     (Rotterdam), 1976 (9th out of 11, 13 points).
Best performances: 1st, weightlifting, cricket, cycling and equal 1st (Hemery) gym-
                     nasium in 1974. 1st, canoeing, shooting, gymnasium (1976
                     European heat).

COOPMAN,   Jean-Pierre (Belgium). Boxing. Born July 11, 1946. Belgian Heavyweight champion since 1972. Nominated challenger to Muhammad Ali after knocking out Britain's Rocky Campbell in 1974. Fought Ali in Puerto Rico in February 1976, and was knocked out.
Superstars record: Belgian heat (Bracknell, G.B.), 1976 (7th, 11 points).
Best performance: 3rd, gymnasium.

DANGUILLAUME,   Jean-Pierre (France). Cycling. Born May 25, 1946 at Jouet les Tours. Signed to ride for Peugot and won bronze medal in the World Pro Road Race championships in Belgium 1975. Had previously competed as an amateur in the 1968 Olympic Games. Won two stages of Tour de France in 1974.
Superstars record: Spanish heat (Aldershot), 1975 (6th, 17.5 points).
Best performance: 2nd, shooting.

DRUT, Guy (France). Athletics. Twenty-seven years old. English mother and lived during childhood in South East London with grandmother. Silver medallist 110 metre hurdles Olympic Games Munich and then won gold medal in same event in Montreal 1976. First athletics gold medal won by a Frenchman for twenty years. European record holder with 13.28 seconds, world manual timed record holder, 13.0 seconds. Banned for life by International Amateur Athletics Federation in 1976 after comments about 'under the counter payments to ahtletes'.

Superstars record: Belgian heat (Bruges), 1975 (champion, 45 points). European final (Rotterdam), 1975 (8th out of 9, 16.50 points). French heat (Vichy), 1976 (runner-up, 45 points). European final (Rotterdam) 1976, (7th out of 11, 16 points).

Best performances: 1st, rowing, soccer penalties, (Belgian heat) 1975.

DUCKHAM, David (G.B.). Rugby Union. Thirty-one years old. British Lion, England and Coventry centre or wing threequarter. 36 caps. Member of first England side to beat the Springboks, December 1969. Injured at end of February 1976 playing for England against Scotland (hamstring and muscle damage), later recovered. Works as a marketing executive in Birmingham. Awarded MBE.

Superstars record; UK National (Aldershot), 1976 (5th out of 10, 23 points).

Best performance: 1st, steeplechase.

DURAN, Jose (Spain). Boxing. Born Madrid October 9, 1945. Spanish Junior Middleweight champion, later won European title (1974). Challenged Miguel de Oliviera for world title 1975 and lost on points. 1976 won world championship. Ex-soccer amateur with Real Madrid.

Superstars record: Belgian heat (Bruges), 1975 (7th, 14 points).

Best performances: 2nd, tennis, steeplechase.

DUVILLARD, Henry (France). Ski-ing. Born December 23, 1947, Megeve. Pro ski-ing's most successful competitor of all-time. In season ending April 1976 has record 15 wins in 21 races to win 66,900 dollars. World champion. As amaetur won World Cup Downhill 1968 and second overall 1971 and 1972. 4th in 1972 Olympic Slalom.

Superstars record: British heat (St. Ives), 1976 (runner-up, 36 points).

Best performance: 1st, weightlifting.

EDWARDS, Gareth Owen (G.B.). Rugby Union. Born July 12, 1947. Welsh international try scoring and appearance record holder and youngest ever captain in 1968 aged twenty years and seven months. British Lion, Cardiff club, scrum-half. First cap 1967. With Lions on first ever defeat of New Zealand on home ground (1971). Engineering works executive and marketing manager. Ex-schoolboy athletics champion (hurdles). Hobby, fly fishing.

Superstars record: UK National (Aldershot), 1976 (4th, 24 points). French heat (Vichy), 1976 (4th, 42.5 points). European final (Rotterdam), 1976 (6th out of 11, 20 points). Note: Competed in only four events due to 'flu'.

Best performances: 1st, weightlifting, soccer skills (UK National). 1st, weightlifting, equal 1st, gymnasium (French heat). 1st, soccer skills (European final).

FERNANDEZ, Pedro 'Perico' (Spain). Boxing. Born November 19, 1952, Zaragoza. Turned professional when seventeen. Won Spanish Light Welterweight title 1972, European 1973 and World title 1974. Lost world title to Saensak Muangsurin of Thailand in Bangkok July 15, 1975.

Superstars record: Dutch heat (Enschede), 1975 (7th, 19 points).

Best performance: 1st, gymnasium.

FIASCONARO, Marcello (Italy). Athletics, Rugby Union. Born July 19, 1949. Son of Italian Air Force pilot who was shot down in North Africa during last war, taken to South Africa as injured prisoner and married Belgian nurse. Fiasconaro born in Belgium, became brilliant rugby threequarter and then 400 metre athlete. 1971 European silver medallist behind Britain's David Jenkins. 1974 broke world record for 800 metres (1:43.7). Achilles tendon injury kept him out of Montreal Olympic Games. Joined Milan as rugby player again. Ex-playboy image, claiming to swallow pint of beer in 3.2 seconds.
Superstars record: Swedish heat (Gothenburg), 1976 (5th, 27.33 points).
Best performances: 1st, swimming, equal 1st, soccer skills.

FITTIPALDI, Emerson (Brazil, resident in Switzerland). Motor Racing. Born São Paulo, Brazil, December 12, 1946. Youngest ever World Drivers' champion at age of twenty-five and 273 days in 1972. Won championship again in 1974. First came to fame with surprise win in 1970 U.S. Grand Prix. Has raced in over 70 Grands Prix.
Superstars record: Dutch heat (Enschede), 1975 (8th out of 8, 15 points).
Best performance: 2nd, cycling.

GALLARDO, Angel (Spain). Golf. Born July 29, 1953 in Barcelona. Turned pro 1962. Won Portugese Open 1967, Spanish 1970, Mexican 1971. Also won Sumrie Better Ball tournament with Maurice Bembridge in 1969 and played for Europe versus G.B. in 1974. Lives in Lausanne, Switzerland where he is the club pro.
Superstars record: Spanish heat (Aldershot), 1975 (7th, 4 points).
Best performance: 4th, shooting.

GARDERUD, Anders (Sweden). Athletics. Born May 28, 1946. World record holder for 3,000 metre steeplechase (8:08.0) and won Olympic gold medal in Montreal 1976. Ran in 800 and 1500 metre heats in Mexico Olympics 1968. Second to Malinowski of Poland in 1974 European championships. Swedish national record holder 1 mile and 5000 metres. P.E. teacher.
Superstars record: Swedish heat (Malmo), 1975 (7th, 16 points).
Best performances: 3rd, soccer skills, swimming and tennis.

GRANATH, Johan (Sweden). Speed Skating. Born March 4, 1950. Won World Sprint Speed Skating title for combined distances of 500 and 1000 metres in West Berlin 1975 after recovering from bad leg injury playing football. Doctors said he would never compete again and was six weeks in plaster. Had 'flu' at Winter Olympic Games in Innsbruck. Has won eight Swedish relay titles, also plays third division football in Sweden. Works as dentist. 6' 3", 13 ½ stone.
Superstars record: Swedish heat (Gothenburg), 1976 (runner-up, 42 points).
European final (Rotterdam), 1976 (equal runner-up, 48 points).
Best performances:1st, cycling (heat). 1st, cycling and steeplechase (final).

GREIG, Anthony William 'Tony' (G.B.). Cricket. Born Queenstown, South Africa, October 6, 1946. England cricket captain, Sussex county captain. Debut for Sussex in 1967, England 1970. 6' 7" tall, 13 stone. One of world's best all-rounders, right hand bat, bowls medium pace. Lead England on 1976-77 tour of India to series win. One of only four England all-rounders to take over 100 wickets and score over 2000 runs in Test matches.
Superstars record: UK National (Crystal Palace), 1974 (4th, 31.5 points).
Best performances: 1st, swimming and football penalties.

HARO, Mariano (Spain). Athletics. Born May 27, 1940. Spain's most successful athlete on track and cross-country. Fifteen years an international. Only 5' 5 ¼" tall,

Finished 4th in Olympic 10,000 metres, Munich after leading with only one lap to go. Placed 6th in Montreal Olympic Games. Runner-up four times in the International Cross Country championships.

Superstars record: Spanish heat (Aldershot), 1975 (5th, 21.5 points). European final (Rotterdam), 1975 (9th out of 9, 3 points).

Best performances: 2nd, cycling and steeplechase (heat).

HEMERY, David Peter (G.B.). Athletics. Born July 18, 1944. Won Olympic gold medal 400 metres hurdles, Mexico 1968, and set world record 48.1 seconds. Lost title and record in Munich 1972 to Akii-Bua of Uganda when Hemery won bronze medal and a silver in the 4 × 400 relay. Commonweath Games gold medallist 1966 and 1970 at 110 metres hurdles and silver medal in 1969 European championships. Moved to Boston, U.S.A. and turned professional. Author of book "Another Hurdle". Awarded MBE.

Superstars record:
1. UK National (Crystal Palace), 1973 (champion, 36 points).
2. UK National (Crystal Palace), 1974 (2nd, 41.83 points).
3. GB heat (Aldershot), 1975 (2nd, 51.5 points).
4. European final (Rotterdam), 1975 (2nd, 39 points).
5. UK National (Aldershot), 1976 (champion, 55.5 points).
6. Swedish heat (Gothenburg), 1976 (3rd, 36.33 points).

Best performances: 1st, swimming, gymnasium, cycle race, steeplechase (see 1 above). 1st, rowing, weightlifting, gymnasium, cycle race (see 3 above). 1st, canoeing, cycle race, shooting, swimming, gymnasium (equal 1st), (see 5 above). 1st, 100 metres, (see 6 above).

HUNT, James Simon Wallis (G.B.). Motor Racing. Born August 29, 1947, Belmont, Surrey. Started motor racing in 1968 in club saloon car races. Formula One in a Hesketh-Surtees 1973 Race of Champions. Previously had had string of crashes in Formula Three and got nick-name "Hunt the Shunt". First Grand Prix Monaco 1973 (9th in March-Ford). First Grand Prix win Holland 1975, placed 4th in World Drivers championship. Changed to Malboro-McLaren and won six Grands Prix and World Drivers championship 1976. Epic duel with Niki Lauda (Austria). Lives at Marbella in Spain. Plays golf, tennis (Junior Wimbledon, 1965) and backgammon. Former trumpeter.

Superstars record: Dutch heat (Enschede), 1975 (3rd, 38 points). UK National (Aldershot), 1976 (3rd, 28 points).

Best performance: 1st, lawn tennis (heat).

ICKX, Jacques Bernard 'Jacky'. (Belgium). Motor Racing. Born New Year's Day, 1945 in Brussels. Former motor cyclist and was Belgian Trials champion for three years. Changed to four wheels and hill-climbing, Saloon Car champion 1965 (Belgium). First Grand Prix: Italian (Cooper-Maserati) 1967, 6th. First Grand Prix win: France (Ferrari) 1968. Runner-up in 1969 and 1970 World Drivers championship. Won Le Mans 1969 and 1975.

Superstars record: GB heat (Aldershot, 1975 (4th, 31 points).

Best performance: 1st, shooting.

ISAKSSON, Kjell (Sweden). Athletics. Aged twenty-eight. P.E. teacher. 5' 8½" which makes him one of the shortest pole-vaulters in world class. One of few men to have cleared 18 feet and has been World Outdoor record holder three times, and Indoor four times. European silver medallist 1968 and 1971. Personal best 5.59 metres in 1972. 10th in Mexico Olympic Games. Father a cyclist, mother a gymnast. Has nightmares of pole "turning into a rope while I am vaulting". Most successful Superstar ever.

Superstars record: 1. Spanish heat (Aldershot), 1975 (champion, 69 points).
2. European final (Rotterdam), 1975 (champion, 56 points).
3. Swedish heat (Gothenburg), 1976 (champion, 66 points).
4. European final (Rotterdam), 1976 (champion, 65 points).
Best performances: 1st, 100 metres, weightlifting, shooting, gymnasium, swimming, steeplechase, (see 1 above). 1st, gymnasium, rowing, weightlifting, steeplechase, (see 2 above). 1st, shooting, weightlifting, canoeing, table tennis, gymnasium, steeplechase, (see 3 above). 1st, swimming, canoeing, gymnasium, table tennis, weightlifting, (see 4 above).

JACKLIN, Tony (G.B.). Golf. Born July 7, 1944, Scunthorpe. Lived near Cheltenham but later moved to tax-exile island of Jersey. Started playing golf when nine, turned professional 1962. Ryder Cup team 1967. Won British Open 1969, US Open 1970. Honorary life president of P.G.A. and awarded OBE. Co-holder of 9-hole record in British Open with 29 strokes in first round at St. Andrews, 1970.
Superstars record: UK National (Crystal Palace), 1973 (7th out of 7, 3.50 points).
Best performance: equal 3rd, cycling.

JOHANNSSON, Kjell (Sweden). Table Tennis. Aged twenty-nine. Won World Doubles championship 1967, 1969 and 1973 when Sweden also won World Team title. Won ten European titles and twenty-five Swedish championships.
Superstars record: Swedish heat (Malmo), 1975 (4th, 35 points).
Best performances: 1st, lawn tennis, steeplechase.

JOHN, Barry (G.B.). Rugby Union. Born 1944. Former student Trinity College, Carmarthen. Welsh international, Llanelli and Cardiff clubs. First cap 1966 versus Australia. Total caps 25. Nicknamed "King John" as Welsh idol. Scored record 188 points on Lions 1971 tour of Australia and New Zealand. Works as a journalist.
Superstars record: UK National (Crystal Palace), 1973 (2nd, 32 points).
Best performances: 1st, 100 metres, lawn tennis, football penalties.

JURION, Joseph 'Jeff' (Belgium). Football. Born 1939. Former Belgian captain with 64 international appearances. Played for Anderlecht and led them to League championship nine times. Midfield player, now coach.
Superstars record: Dutch heat (Enschede), 1975 (6th, 21 points).
Best performance: 1st, 100 metres.

KEEGAN, Kevin (G.B.). Football. Born February 14, 1951. 5' 8" tall. Comes from Doncaster in Yorkshire. England international and Liverpool. "Footballer of the Year" award. Joined Liverpool from Scunthorpe (where he started as apprentice at sixteen) for only £33,000 after four seasons. Scored two goals in the 1973-74 Cup final to help beat Newcastle United 3-0. Made over 300 league appearances and scored over 70 goals in career.
Superstars record: Belgian heat (Bracknell, G.B.), 1976 (champion, 54 points).
Best performances: 1st, canoeing, weightlifting, steeplechase.

KILLY, Jean-Claude (France). Ski-ing. Born August 30, 1943. At 1968 Winter Olympic Games, Grenoble, won all three Alpine events, the downhill, slalom and giant slalom. Won World Cup 1967 and 1968. Turned professional after one of greatest amateur winter sports careers of all time. Became world pro champion 1973. Lives in Geneva and made film debut in 1974.
Superstars record: Spanish heat (Aldershot, G.B.), 1975 (3rd, 39 points).
Best performances: 1st, rowing, cycling.

KLAMMER, Franz (Austria). Ski-ing. Born December 3, 1953. Greatest downhiller of all time. Won gold medal in Innsbruck, 1976 Winter Olympic Games. Retained World Cup title (which he'd first won in 1974-75 season) and won eight downhill races, breaking speed records every time. Member of Austrian team since 1973 and year later won alpine combination gold medal at St. Mortiz in world championships, second in the downhill. Hobbies, moto-cross, horse-riding and sailing.
Superstars record: Belgian heat (Bracknell, G.B.), 1976 (4th, 41.50 points).
Best performances: 1st, gymnasium, cycling.

KLEINE, Piet (Holland). Speed Skating. Born 1952. Lives at Hollandscheveld near Danish border. Postman. Won gold medal 10,000 metres and silver 5000 metres at Winter Olympic Games, Innsbruck, 1976 and was 6th in 1500 metres. World champion for combined distances of 10,000 and 5000 metres. Set world record for 5000 metres in March 1976 with a time of 7:02.38.
Superstars record: G.B. heat (St. Ives), 1976 (8th out of 8, 16.50 points).
Best performance: 1st, cycling.

KROL, Ruud, 'Rudi' (Holland). Football. Born March 24, 1949. Captain of Ajax joining them in 1968. First international cap 1969, regular member of their World Cup team in 1974 when Holland were runners-up to West Germany, beaten 2-1 in the Munich final. Sweeper. Played over forty European Cup matches for Ajax but sat on touch-line for their first, against Panathinaikos at Wembley, with a broken leg. Member of side that won European Cup in 1972 and 1973. Lives at Zaandam and owns several shops in Amsterdam.
Superstars record: Belgian heat (Bracknell, G.B.), 1976 (45.5 points). European final (Rotterdam), 1976 (5th, 24 points).
Best performances: 1st, table tennis (heat). 2nd, table tennis (final).

KRUIZE, Ties (Holland). Hockey. Born November 17, 1952. Member of Dutch hockey side since 1971, played in World championships that year and in 1973 and 1975. Centre-forward and was top individual goal scorer in Olympic Games, Munich 1972 with eighteen goals. Holland finished 4th. Son of famous Dutch hockey player who competed in 1948 and 1952 Olympic Games. Uses an unusually heavy stick. Badly injured in a car crash during the 1975 European Superstars series and unable to take his place in the final.
Superstars record: G.B. heat (Aldershot), 1975 (champion, 56 points).
Best performances: 1st, 100 metres, swimming, lawn tennis.

KUIPER, Hennie (Holland). Cycling. Born February 3, 1949. Student of languages (fluent in English, French, German and Dutch) and a student of engineering. Won English Milk Race and Olympic Games 1972 later turning professional. Joined West German Rokado team, then Holland's Fristol team and won World Road Racing championship in Belgium. Moved again to TR Raleigh and became team captain. Stage winner Tour de France in which he retired injured and went to hospital.
Superstars record: French heat (Vichy), 1976 (5th, 25.5 points).
Best performance: 1st, shooting.

KUIPERS, Harm (Holland). Speed skating. Born 1948, started skating at age of four, in competitions from the age of nineteen. Won world title 1975 after two Dutch National championships and second place in European championships (1975). Natural successor to his fellow countryman, Ard Schenk. Did not compete in Winter Olympic Games, Innsbruck, 1976, as he was in final year of medical studies. Former cyclist. Lives in Haren-Groeningen.

Superstars record: Swedish heat (Malmo), 1975 (equal 2nd, 45 points). European final (Rotterdam), 1975 (6th, 20 points).
Best performances: 1st cycling (heat). 1st, cycling (final).

LITJENS,   Paul (Holland). Hockey. Born November 1947. Lawyer. 6' tall, 14 stone 2 lbs. Top scorer in Montreal Olympic Hockey tournament 1976 with eleven goals and scored both goals when Holland were beaten 3-2 by Pakistan in 3rd/4th place play-off. Played with Ties Kruize (see above) in Munich Olympics when Holland again just missed a medal. Made international debut 1970 and has over 60 caps. Member of Dutch team that won world title in 1973.
Superstars record: Dutch heat (Vlaardingen), 1976 (equal 3rd, 32 points).
Best performance: 1st, 100 metres.

MACDONALD,   Malcolm (G.B.). Football. Born January 7, 1950 in London. Reserve full-back with Fulham, moved to Luton Town as striker, transferred to Newcastle for £180,000. England international (first cap 1972 versus Wales) and equalled England's top scoring record (versus Cyprus at Wembley 1975) with five individual goals. Joined Arsenal for 1976-77 season. To end of 1975-76 season had made over 280 league appearances scoring 149 goals. Nicknamed "Supermac". Fastest Superstar ever in Europe.
Superstars record: 1. Swedish heat (Malmo), 1975 (champion, 48 points).
                               2. European final (Rotterdam), 1975 (7th, 18.50 points).
                               3. UK National (Aldershot), 1976 (equal 8th, 16 points).
Best performances: 1st, 100 metres, shooting, weightlifting, (see 1 above). 1st, 100 metres, (see 2 above). 1st, 100 metres, (see 3 above).

MAERTENS,   Freddie (Belgium). Cycling. Born February 13, 1952. In 1973 runner-up in World Road Race championship in San Sebastian to Gimondo of Spain with his fellow countryman Eddy Merckx third. Has won Tour of Andalucia, Tour of Luxembourg, Tour of Belgium and had excellent season 1976. Eight stage victories in Tour de France to equal record and finished 8th overall. Won World Professional Road Race title, and in the 1972 Olympic Games, Munich had gained 13th place in road race.
Superstars record: Belgian heat (Bruges), 1975 (8th out of 8, 13 points).
Best performance: 2nd, football penalties.

MAERTENS,   Maurice (Belgium). Football. Born June 5, 1947. Started professional football career with Anderlecht, then moved to Racing White Daring of Molenbeek. Left-back and Belgian international. Member of their 1970 world cup squad in Mexico. In 1974 won two of top awards in Belgium — the Golden Shoe for the best player and La Trophée du Profit de Mèrite, the Press Award. Cartilage operation in 1975. Lives at Aalst and owns a sports shop.
Superstars record: G.B. heat (St. Ives), 1976 (7th, 19 points).
Best performances: 3rd, table tennis, swimming, shooting, cycling.

MAGNUSSON,   Thomas (Sweden). Ski-ing. Born Motala, July 2, 1950. Ex-soccer goalkeeper, turned to cross-country ski-ing winning string of national titles at 15, 30 and 50 kms. Won World 30 km title at Falun in 1974 but in Winter Olympic Games, Innsbruck 1976, he had to fly home just before he was due to compete following the death of his father in a road accident. Lives at Stockholm, works for a sports goods company.
Superstars record: G.B. heat (St. Ives), 1976 (5th, 29.50 points).
Best performances: 1st, table tennis, swimming.

MARTINELLI, Guiseppe (Italy). Cycling. Born March 11, 1955. 5' 8½'' tall. Competed in the Olympic Games in Montreal in 1976 and won the silver medal in the road race.
Superstars record: French heat (Vichy), 1976 (6th, 15 points).
Best performance: 2nd, swimming.

MASS, Jochen (West Germany). Motor Racing. Born September 30, 1946 in Cologne. First Grand Prix — British 1973 when he was involved in a first lap incident in his Surtees. First Grand Prix victory — Spanish, 1975 when he was leading and the race was stopped after an accident. 3rd three times in French, US, and Brazilian races and that year 8th in World Drivers championship, won by Niki Lauda. Top driver to come from Germany since the late Taffy Von Tripps.
Superstars record: Swedish heat (Malmo), 1975 (equal 2nd, 45 points). European final (Rotterdam), 1976 (4th, 30 points).
Best performances: 1st, swimming, gymnasium (heat). 1st, swimming (final).

MATHY, François (Belgium). Show jumping. Born on New Year's Eve, 1944. Started competition when he was sixteen, took Belgian national title three times and went to Montreal for Olympic Games 1976. Rode *Gai Luron* and won individual bronze medal, just beating Debbie Johnsey of G.B., and was member of Belgian team that won the other bronze medal. Has won Grands Prix in Paris, Berlin and Limoges. Also rode in Munich Games 1972. Lives at Louveigne. Wife's father was one of Belgium's top all-round sportsmen, Raymond Lambert.
Superstars record: Swedish heat (Gothenburg), 1976 (7th, 6.33 points).
Best performances: 4th, weightlifting, steeplechase.

MICHANEK, Anders (Sweden). Speedway. Born May 1943, began career with Swedish second division club, Gamarna and moved to Getingarna of Stockholm. Came to England in 1967 riding for Long Eaton, Leciester, Newcastle and Reading. Won world championship 1974, World Pairs 1973, 1974 and 1975, team 1970. First speedway rider to compete in Superstars. Left English clubs to resume riding in Stockholm at end of 1975 season to spend more time with family.
Superstars record: Dutch heat (Vlaardingen), 1976 (2nd, 38 points).
Best performances: 1st, cycling, shooting, canoeing.

MORELON, Daniel (France). Cycling. Born July 28, 1944 at Bourg-en-Brasse. Rated as one of the greatest champions ever. Has won medals at four successive Olympic Games — Tokyo 1964, bronze individual sprint; Mexico City, golds in individual and tandem; Munich, gold individual; Montreal (on eve of 32nd birthday) silver medal individual. Seven times a world champion, thirteen times French champion, world record holder indoor amateur unpaced 200 metres with flying start, 1967, 10.72 seconds.
Superstars record: Swedish heat (Gothenburg), 1976 (8th out of 8, 4.33 points).
Best performances: 5th, table-tennis, swimming, soccer skills, steeplechase.

MOORE, Robert Frederick 'Bobby' (G.B.). Football. Born Barking, April 12, 1941. 6' 0'', 12 stone 13 lbs. England, West Ham and Fulham. Former England Youth and under-23 captain. First England cap 1962 versus Peru. Captain of West Ham when they won FA Cup 1964 and of England for 1966 World Cup win. Also captained England in 1970 World Cup. Record 108 caps 1962-73. To the end of the 1975-76 season had made 628 league appearances and scored 25 goals. Awarded OBE.
Superstars record: UK National (Crystal Palace), 1973 (6th, 8 points).
Best performance: 2nd, swimming.

NEUREUTHER, Christian (West Germany). Ski-ing. Born April 28, 1949. Slalom specialist and has won eleven national titles since 1968. 2nd in overall

standings for World Cup Slalom in 1973 and 1974, and won four world cup races outright in the two seasons. Medical student in Munich and a former world student ski champion (1972). Lives in Garmisch, home of the famous New Year's Day ski-jump event. Races saloon cars at top level. In Innsbruck for 1976 Winter Olympic Games was 5th in Slalom and 30th in Giant Slalom.
Superstars record: G.B. heat (St. Ives), 1976 (4th, 31.50 points).
Best performance: 1st, soccer skills.

NIETO, Angel, 'El Nino' (Spain). Motor Cycling. Born 1947, Zamora. Youngest winner of World 50 cc title in 1969 when only twenty-two. Has won four 50 cc and two 125 cc world titles at road racing. Won 1975 50 cc title riding German built Kreidler machine for Dutch sponsors. Approaching half-century of world championship race victories.
Superstars record: Swedish heat (Malmo), 1975 (8th out of 8, 8 points).
Best performance: 2nd, football penalties.

NORDQVIST, Bjorn (Sweden). Football. Born October 6, 1942. International debut versus Hungary in 1963 and went on to win over 80 caps and become Swedish captain. Legendary figure in football. Played against Yugoslavia in European championship last season and has now completed three years with Dutch club P.S.V. Eindhoven, moving back to own country to play for E.S.K. Goteburg.
Superstars record: G.B. heat (Aldershot), 1975 (5th, 30 points).
Best performances: 2nd, rowing, weightlifting.

NUSSE, Frank (Holland). Athletics. Born March 23, 1953. 400 metres hurdler and in 1975 set new Dutch record of 49.48 which would have won the Olympic bronze medal in Montreal the following year; but he'd been ruled out by a foot injury. Began career as decathlete and won bronze medal in European Youth championships 1970. Dutch 400 metres hurdles champion 1973, also won 110 and 200 metres hurdles and 3rd place in A.A.A. 400 metres hurdles in 1975. Medical student in Amsterdam and won Dutch National Superstar title.
Superstars record: Swedish heat (Gothenburg), 1976 (4th, 35.33 points). European final (Rotterdam), 1976 (4th, 38 points).
Best performances: 2nd, 100 metres, table tennis (heat). 2nd, 100 metres, swimming (final).

OKKER, Tom (Holland). Lawn Tennis. Born February 22, 1944 in Amsterdam. Holland's greatest ever tennis player, known as "The Flying Dutchman" for speed around the court. Won a string of major titles including South African, Italian, Belgian, Dutch and German championships. Signed with World Championship of Tennis and has very good doubles record with Marty Riessen winning the 1976 US title to add to their many championships. Lives in Switzerland.
Superstars record: Spanish heat (Aldershot, G.B.), 1975 (4th, 29 points).
Best performances: 2nd, swimming, football penalties.

OSTARCEVIC, Marco (France). Basketball. Born 1941 in Yugoslavia. Former international high jumper and football centre forward, also ranked tennis player. Naturalised Frenchman in 1973 and now one of Europe's leading basketball attackers. Captain of Racing Club de France and an amateur. 6' 1" tall but is the shortest member of the team. Lives in Paris.
Superstars record: Belgian heat (Bracknell, G.B.), 1976 (3rd, 45 points). European final (Rotterdam), 1976 (11th out of 11, 8.50 points).
Best performances: 1st, soccer skills, swimming, shooting (heat). 3rd, swimming (final).

PASCOE, Alan Peter (G.B.). Athletics. Born October 11, 1947 in Portsmouth. 6' 1½", 11½ stone. European 400 metres hurdles champion Rome 1974, Commonwealth champion Christchurch, New Zealand 1974, Europa Cup winner Nice 1975, Olympic Silver medallist 4 × 400 1972, European gold medal 4 × 400 1974, Commonwealth silver medal 4 × 400 1974. At 110 metres hurdles has won European silver (1971), bronze (1969). Reached Montreal Olympic Games finals in 1976 and placed 8th (400 metres hurdles). Ranked world number 1 in 1976, now working in public relations. Eleven times A.A.A. champion including indoor. Awarded MBE.
Superstars record: Belgian heat (Bruges), 1975 (3rd, 39.50 points).
Best performance: 1st, shooting.

PIETRANGELI, Nicola (Italy). Lawn Tennis. Born September 11, 1933, Tunis. Russian mother and French father. One of finest hard court players in world at end of 1950's when he won French title twice running. First Davis Cup in 1954 and by the end of 1972 had competed in 164 rubbers, winning 119, in 66 ties, a Davis Cup record. Has won 24 Italian titles, Wimbledon semi-finalist in 1960. Good soccer player and awarded Italian gold medal for athletic valour in 1965.
Superstars record: G.B. heat (Aldershot), 1975 (6th, 17 points).
Best performance: 1st, football penalties.

POULIDOR, Raymond "Pou-Pou" (France). Cycling. France's sporting legend. Born April 15, 1936. First big win 1959 at Louvain. Following year was 5th in World Road Race championship. Two years later was French champion and since has won almost everything except the Tour de France. In ths he has been 2nd twice, 3rd four times, once in 1976 at the age of forty, his 15th Tour. Awarded Chevalier de Legion d'Honneur.
Superstars record: French heat (Vichy), 1976 (8th out of 8, 3 points).
Best performances: 5th, 100 metres, weightlifting, gymnasium.

REXACH, Carlos (Spain). Football. Born 1949. With F.C. Barcelonia since he was a boy. Plays as winger on either flank and has reputation as "Hardest shot in Spanish football". Regular international and was captain of his country against Scotland in the European championship at the end of the 1974-75 season. Also played for Barcelona versus Leeds United in two dramatic semi-final European Cup matches.
Superstars record: G.B. heat (Aldershot), 1975 (7th out of 8, 14 points).
Best performance: 2nd, lawn tennis.

RITTER, Ole (Denmark). Cycling. Born August 29, 1941. Denmark's number 1 cyclist who won the "Blue Riband" event, the world one hour record, in 1968. He held it until it went to Eddie Merckx in 1972. Mainly a track-racer, has held world record 5 km and 100 km.
Superstars record: Belgian heat (Bracknell, G.B.), 1976 (8th out of 8, 7 points).
Best performance: 3rd, soccer skills.

RUSSI, Bernard (Switzerland). Ski-ing. Born August 20, 1948, Andermatt. Olympic gold medal for downhill in 1972 and silver for same event in Innsbruck (1976). Has also won 1970 World Downhill title and is now one of the oldest skiers on the world cup circuit. World Cup Downhill champion 1971 and 1972.
Superstars record: G.B. heat (St. Ives), 1976 (3rd, 35 points).
Best performance: 1st, 100 metres.

SALMING, Borje (Sweden). Ice Hockey. Born April 17, 1951. 6' 1'', 13 stone 8 lbs. One of the finest ice-hockey players to come from Sweden. Began with Brynas

Club and appeared many times in Swedish national team. Went to Canada early 1970s and was voted best non-American defenceman in the game. Signed one-million-dollar three year contract with Toronto Maple Leafs and voted to National Hockey League All-Star Number Two team.

Superstars record: Dutch heat (Enschede), 1975 (2nd, 45 points).
Best performances: 1st, weightlifting, swimming.

SCHECKTER, Jody (South African, resident in Spain). Motor Racing. Born in East London, South Africa January 29, 1950. Lives in Marbella, Spain. First Grand Prix United States 1972 when he finished 9th in a McLaren. First win, Sweden 1974. In 1973 in the British Grand Prix was involved in the spectacular multi-car crash at Silverstone. Won the event at Brands Hatch in 1974 and took 3rd place in World Drivers championship. Won South African Grand Prix 1975 and following year signed for new Wolf team winning one Grand Prix and finishing second in four others.

Superstars record: Belgian heat (Bruges), 1976 (4th, 38 points).
Best performances: 1st, swimming, gymnasium.

SCHENK, Andrianus 'Ard' (Holland). Speed-Skating. Born September 16, 1944, 6' 2¾", 14 stone 2 lbs. Won three gold medals — 1,500, 5000 and 10,000 metres in the 1972 Winter Olympic Games in Sapporo, Japan. Set Olympic records for 1,500 and 10,000 metres. Won first European title in 1971 after taking silver medal in 1968 Olympic 1,500 metres. Set up new world record in 1972 for 3000 metres (4:08.30) having previously held world records for 1,500, 5000 and 10,000 metres. Turned pro and took part in 1974 US Superstars, won Dutch Superstars in 1975. Physiotherapist, lives in Amstelveen.

Superstars record: Dutch heat (Enschede), 1975 (champion, 47 points). European final (Rotterdam), 1975 (3rd, 36 points).
Best performances: 1st, cycling, football penalties, steeplechase (heat). 1st, shooting, football penalties (final).

SCHNABL, Karl (Austria). Ski Jumping. Born March 8, 1954. Won Olympic gold medal on 90 metre ski jump in Innsbruck, 1976 and bronze on the 70 metre. First success only year before when he won the Four-hills tournament and the jumps at Lathi in Finland, Sapporo in Japan, and a bronze medal in the World Ski-Flying championships. Farmer's son from Achomitz and is reading Philosophy and sport at Innsbruck University. Lost form after Olympic Games and withdrew after two days of the 1977 World Ski-Flying championships in Norway.

Superstars record: Dutch heat (Vlaardingen), 1976 (champion, 47 points). European final (Rotterdam), 1976 (equal 2nd, 48 points).
Best performances: 1st, weightlifting, swimming, gymnasium (heat). 1st, shooting (final).

SHILTON, Peter (G.B.). Football. Born September 18, 1949. International goalkeeper at all-levels (schoolboy, youth, under-23 and full cap). Began pro career with Leicester City and appeared in the team that lost to Manchester City in the 1969 Cup final. Helped them win promotion to Division One in 1970-71. November 1974 transferred to Stoke City for a fee of £300,000 setting world record for a goalkeeper. First England cap versus East Germany in 1971. Celebrated 21st appearance for England in 1975 versus Cyprus.

Superstars record: G.B. heat (St. Ives), 1976 (6th, 27 points).
Best performance 1st, steeplechase.

SNOEK, Hendrik (West Germany). Show Jumping. Born Munster April 2, 1948.

Riding since he was twelve, in Nations Cup team at nineteen and won British Jumping Derby at Hickstead in Sussex (one of world's major outdoor events) in 1972. Regular member of Germany's President's Cup winning team. Graduated as an economist and was reserve in Montreal Olympic Games.
Superstars record: Dutch heat (Enschede), 1975 (4th, 31 points).
Best performance: 1st, shooting.

SPANGHERO, Walter (France). Rugby Union. Born August 21, 1943. 6' 2½", approximately 16 stone. One of the biggest men in French rugby. Won first of over 50 caps in 1964. Plays at forward in variety of positions and his brother Claude is a fellow-international. Farmer's son, manages a car-hire business in Toulouse. Married in 1976 and over 500 guests turned up at the party in his father's farmhouse and it lasted all night. Took part in Superstars during his honeymoon.
Superstars record: Dutch heat (Vlaardingen), 1976 (8th out of 8, 13 points).
Best performances: 3rd, shooting, soccer skills.

STARBROOK, David Colin (G.B.). Judo. Born August 9, 1945. 6' 1", 13 stone 13 lbs. Won silver medal at light-heavyweight in Olympic Games, Munich and bronze in Montreal, 1976. Formed part of Britain's most successful ever judo trio (Keith Remfrey and Brian Jacks the others). Won medals at National, European and World level and the silver in Munich was Britain's first Olympic medal of any kind in the sport. Holds record nine British championships. Medal record: Gold—European championships 1971, team; Silver—Olympic 1972, European Individual 1973 and 1974, team 1974; Bronze—Olympic 1976, World Individual 1971 and 1973, European Individual 1974 and 1975, team 1976. Retired after Montreal. Awarded MBE.
Superstars record: UK National (Aldershot), 1976 (6th, 21.50 points).
Best performance: equal 1st, gymnasium.

STENSEN, Sten (Norway). Speed-Skating. Born December 18, 1947. Olympic gold medal in Innsbruck 1976 for 5000 metres and silver at 10,000 metres. Four years before won bronze at both distances in Sapporo, Japan. Started skating seriously in 1966 and became World champion in 1974, European champion 1975. Was runner-up in the 1976 World championships and set world record for 10,000 metres (14:38.08). Lieutenant in Norwegian Army. Second of two daughters born during the Innsbruck Olympic Games.
Superstars record: Swedish heat (Gothenburg), 1976 (6th, 22.33 points).
Best performance: equal 1st, soccer skills.

STEVENIERS, Willi (Belgium). Basketball. Born 1938. Top player in Belgium. Made his name with Aaslt Club but later joined American based Belgium Lions—only European in this predominantly American Negro team. Nicknamed "The Emperor", plays left wing. Over 50 international caps and many times in All-Europe team.
Superstars record: Swedish heat (Malmo), 1975 (5th, 22 points).
Best performance: 3rd, rowing.

STEWART, Jackie (G.B.). Motor Racing. Born in Milton, Dunbartonshire, June 11, 1939. Started racing 1961. In 1964 won twelve of fourteen races to become European Formula Three champion. In first Formula One season, won Italian Grand Prix and was 3rd in World Drivers championship. Won title in 1969, 1971 and 1973 when he retired with record 27 wins in 99 Grand Prix races. Champion clay pigeon shot, now business man and television commentator. Awarded OBE.
Superstars record: UK National (Crystal Palace), 1973 (equal 3rd, 25 points).
Best performance: 1st, golf.

STRACEY, John Henry (G.B.). Boxing. Born Bethnal Green, September 22, 1950. Amateur champion at light welterweight 1969 and had first pro fight September 17 that year when he beat Santos Martins, k.o. 2nd round, Bethnal Green. British champion 1972 (welterweight), European champion 1974 and won World title in December 1975, beating José Napoles in Mexico in 6th round. Lost title in 1976.
Superstars record: UK National (Crystal Palace), 1974 (5th, 24.33 points).
Best performances: 2nd, swimming, cricket.

TAYLOR, Roger (G.B.). Lawn Tennis. Born October 14, 1941 in Sheffield. Three times Wimbledon semi-finalist—1967, 1970 and 1973. Turned professional with W.C.T. in 1968 when they formed the "Handsome Eight". Featured in the famous 1973 boycott of Wimbledon by A.T.P. when he refused to support the ban (along with Ilie Nastase) and beat Bjorn Borg to reach semi-final for third time, losing to Kodes, the eventual champion. Same year became first British player to reach W.C.T. finals, losing to Ken Rosewall in epic match. Useful soccer and squash player.
Superstars record: UK National (Crystal Palace), 1973 (5th, 10.50 points).
Best performance: 2nd, 100 metres.

VAN BINST, Gilbert (Belgium). Football. Born July 1951. Captain of National team 15 times. Led Anderlecht to national titles and to European Cup Winners' Cup final victory over West Ham in 1976 (4-2 in Brussels). Plays right defence.
Superstars record: Belgian heat (Bracknell, G.B.), 1976 (5th, 20 points).
Best performance: 1st, 100 metres.

VAN DAMME, Ivo (Belgium). Athletics. Born February 21, 1954. Died December 29, 1976. Began serious athletics in 1972 and soon established himself as Belgium's best 800 metres runner since Roger Moens. Finished fourth to Britain's Steve Ovett in the 1973 European Junior championships but 'flu upset his career and he was out for a season. In 1974-75 won silver medal in European Indoor championships followed by gold in Munich 1976. In Montreal Olympic Games won silver medal in both 800 and 1,500 metres. Fatally injured in car crash in France on December 29, 1976 when driving home to watch the European final of Superstars on television in which he'd taken part.
Superstars record: French heat (Vichy), 1976 (3rd, 44 points). European final
                     (Rotterdam), 1976 (10th out of 11, 12.50 points).
Best performances: 1st, 100 metres, swimming, cycling (heat). 1st, 100 metres
                     (final).

VAN HANEGEM, Wim (Holland). Football. Born February 22, 1944. Played for Velox and then Xerxes of Rotterdam. Moved to Feyenoord where he's been for eight seasons as a mid-field player. Member of team that won European Cup in 1970 beating Celtic 2-1 and of U.E.F.A. Cup winning side in 1974. Regular Dutch international and world cup player. Good tennis player.
Superstars record: Dutch heat (Vlaardingen), 1976 (7th, 21 points).
Best performance: 1st, table tennis.

VAN HIMST, Paul (Belgium). Football. Born October 2, 1943. Captain of national team with Belgian record of 81 caps. Joined Anderlecht in 1959-60 season at age of sixteen. Helped them to win eight League titles, (five in a row) and Belgian Cup four times. Four times Player of The Year. Moved from Anderlecht in 1976 to Racing White Daring of Molenbeek, causing transfer sensation.
Superstars record: Belgian heat (Bruges), 1975 (2nd, 41 points).
Best performances: 1st, steeplechase, 100 metres, cycling.

VAN LENNEP, Gijs (Holland). Motor Racing. Born March 16, 1942. Won 1971 Le Mans 24 Hour Race, European Formula 5,000 1973 and Targa Floria 1973. Won Le Mans again in 1976 and holds record (with co-driver Helmut Marko) with 3,315.2 miles in 1971 race.
Superstars record: Dutch heat (Enschede), 1975 (5th, 23 points).
Best performance: 1st, rowing.

WILKIE, David Andrew (G.B.). Swimming. Born March 8, 1954. In Montreal Olympic Games, 1976 became first British Swimmer to win gold medal since 1908 when he won 200 metre breaststroke in new world record time (2:15.11). Won silver medal for 100 metres in same games and had won silver for 200 metres four years previously in Munich. Retired after games having won every major title—World, European Commonwealth and Olympic. Now sports master at public school. Awarded MBE.
Superstars record: Dutch heat (Vlaardingen), 1976 (6th, 28 points).
Best performance: 1st, soccer skills.

WILLIAMS, John P.R. (G.B.). Rugby Union. Born March 2, 1949 in Bridgend, Wales. Became Wimbledon Junior Tennis Champion 1966 but turned to Rugby and won first cap in 1969 while playing for London Welsh (and qualifying as a doctor). British Lion (1971 and 1974). Record number of caps by a full back for Wales (37 to end of 1976 season). Returned briefly to tennis in 1970 to reach final of National under-21 championships. Former member of Welsh National Youth Orchestra, violin. Ranked as world's greatest full-back.
Superstars record: UK National (Aldershot), 1976 (equal 8th, 16 points).
Best performance: 1st, lawn tennis.

ZOETEMELK, Joop (Holland). Cycling. Born December 3, 1946 in The Hague. Best known name in Dutch cycling. 1975 retained title in Paris-Nice race, finishing ahead of Eddy Merckx, 4th in Tour de France. In 1976 won two stages of Tour de France, finishing 2nd overall as in 1970 and 1971. Placed 3rd in 1976 World Super Prestige championship. Lives near Meaux in France.
Superstars record: Belgian heat (Bruges), 1975 (6th, 15 points).
Best performance: 2nd, shooting.

SUPERSTARS RESULTS
Rotunda, Florida, USA 1973 BBC 1 T.V. TXN April 23 1973

Competitors
Johnny Bench (Baseball)
Jean-Claude Killy (Ski-ing)
Rod Laver (Lawn Tennis)
Bob Seagren (Athletics)
Elvin Hayes (Basketball)
Joe Frazier (Boxing)
Rod Gilbert (Ice Hockey)
Peter Revson (Motor Racing)
Jim Stefanich (Bowling)
Johnny Unitas (American Football)
Points system: Win 10 points, 2nd 7 points, 3rd 4 points, 4th 2 points, 5th 1 point.
Prize money: Total 122,000 US dollars.
Each competitor $300 for every point gained.
Final bonus: Winner $25,000, 2nd $15,000, 3rd $10,000.
Events: Total 10. Each competitor chose 7, barred from speciality.

Final result

1	Bob Seagren	49 points ($14,700), win bonus $25,000, extra bonuses $8,500. Total prize money $48,200.
2	Jean-Claude Killy	28 points ($8,400), bonus $15,000. Total prize money $23,400.
3 {	Peter Revson	27 points ($8,100), share 3rd place, bonus $5,000. Total prize money $13,100.
	Rod Laver	27 points $13,100.
5	Johnny Bench	26 points $7,800.
6	Elvin Hayes	24 points $7,200.
7 {	Rod Gilbert	17½ points $5,250.
	Jim Stefanich	17½ points $5,250.
9 {	Joe Frazier	12 points $3,600.
	Johnny Unitas	12 points $3,600.

Event results

Swimming (100 metres)
1 Peter Revson 1 min. 18.2 secs.
2 Bob Seagren
3 Jean-Claude Killy

Lawn Tennis
Peter Revson beat Rod Gilbert 6-1

Cycle race (1 mile)
1 Bob Seagren 3:19.05
2 Rod Laver
3 Jean-Claude Killy

Golf (nine holes)
1 Jim Stefanich 41 shots
2 Johnny Bench 42 shots
3 Rod Laver

Bowling (ten-pin)
1 Johnny Bench 131
2 Johnny Unitas 124
3 Elvin Hayes 123

Weightlifting
1 Bob Seagren 170 lbs.
2 Joe Frazier 160 lbs.
3 { Jean-Claude Killy / Peter Revson } 140 lbs.

100 yards
1 Elvin Hayes 11.5 secs.
2 Jean-Claude Killy
3 Rod Laver

Baseball Hitting
1 Bob Seagren
2 { Jim Stefanich / Rod Gilbert

Table Tennis
Rod Laver beat Jean-Claude Killy 11-0

Half-mile
1 Bob Seagren 2:22.5
2 Elvin Hayes
3 Johnny Bench

UK NATIONAL SUPERSTARS, August 20th and 21st 1973
Crystal Palace and Sundridge Park Golf Club, Bromley

Competitors
Jackie Stewart (Motor Racing)
Tony Jacklin (Golf)
Barry John (Rugby Union)
Joe Bugner (Boxing)
Roger Taylor (Tennis)
David Hemery (Athletics)
Bobby Moore (Football)

Points system: Each competitor chooses eight events out of ten. Win 7 points, 2nd 4 points, 3rd 2 points, 4th 1 point.

Prize money: Winner £4,000, 2nd £2,500, 3rd £1,500.

Overall result

1	David Hemery	36 points
2	Barry John	32 points
3 {	Joe Bugner	25 points
}	Jackie Stewart	25 points
5	Roger Taylor	10½ points
6	Bobby Moore	8 points
7	Tony Jacklin	3½ points

Event results

	Event points	Running total	Overall position
100 metres			
1 Barry John	7	7	1
2 Roger Taylor	4	4	2
3 Jackie Stewart	2	2	3
4 Joe Bugner	1	1	4
Air pistol shooting			
(five clay discs from 10 metres)			
1 Joe Bugner	7	8	1
2 Jackie Stewart	4	6	3
3 David Hemery	2	2	5
4 Tony Jacklin	1	1	6
50 metre Swim			
1 David Hemery	7	9	2
2 Bobby Moore	4	4	=5
3 Joe Bugner	2	10	1
4 Barry John	1	8	3
Golf (three holes, par 3, 4, 5)			
1 Jackie Stewart*	7	13	1
2 Barry John	4	12	2
3 Roger Taylor	2	6	5
4 Bobby Moore	1	5	6
*(after play-off)			
Gymnasium tests			
1 David Hemery	7	16	1
2 Joe Bugner	4	14	=2
3 Barry John	2	14	=2
4 Jackie Stewart	1	14	=2

Lawn Tennis			
1 Barry John	7	21	1
2 Jackie Stewart	4	18	2
3 Bobby Moore	2	7	5
4 Tony Jacklin	1	2	7

Football (6 shots from penality spot versus Pat Jennings, Spurs and Northern Ireland International). (Barry John and Joe Bugner each scored 3 goals and in a kick-off, Barry John scored with first attempt with Bugner missing).

1 Barry John	7	28	1
2 Joe Bugner	4	18	=3
3 David Hemery	2	18	=3
4 Jackie Stewart	1	19	2

Cycle racing (800 metres, track)

1 David Hemery	7	25	2
2 Jackie Stewart	4	23	3
3 {Tony Jacklin	1.50	3.50	7
{Roger Taylor	1.50	7.50	5

Weightlifting

1 Joe Bugner	7	25	=3
2 David Hemery	4	29	1
3 Jackie Stewart	2	25	=3
4 Roger Taylor	1	8.50	5

600 metres Steeplechase
(on handicap)

1 David Hemery	7	36	1
2 Barry John	4	32	2
3 Roger Taylor	2	10.50	5
4 Bobby Moore	1	8	6

U.K. NATIONAL SUPERSTARS 1974, July 22nd and 23rd.
Crystal Palace

Competitors
Mike Channon (Football)
Tony Greig (Cricket)
John Conteh (Boxing)
John H. Stracey (Boxing)
Chay Blyth (Yachting)
Colin Bell (Football)
David Hemery (Athletics) Defending champion

Points system: Each competitor chooses 8 events from the list of 10. Win 10 points, 2nd 7 points, 3rd 4 points, 4th 2 points, 5th 1 point.

Prize money: Winner £4,000, 2nd £2,500, 3rd £1,500, 4th £1,000.

Overall result

1	John Conteh	57.83 points
2	David Hemery	41.83 points
3	Colin Bell	41 points
4	Tony Greig	31.50 points
5	John H. Stracey	24.33 points
6	Chay Blyth	22.50 points
7	Mike Channon	21 points

Event results

		Event points	Running total	Overall position
100 metres				
1	Mike Channon	10	10	1
2	John Conteh	7	7	2
3	Colin Bell	4	4	3
4	Tony Greig	2	2	4
5	J. H. Stracey	1	1	5
Weightlifting				
1	John Conteh (95 kgs)	10	17	1
2	David Hemery (87½ kgs)	7	7	3
3	J. H. Stracey	4	5	5
4	Colin Bell	2	6	4
5	Chay Blyth	1	1	7
Pistol Shooting				
(air-pistols and clay discs)				
1	Colin Bell	10	16	2
2 {	Chay Blyth	5.50	6.50	6
{	Tony Greig	5.50	7.50	5
4	David hemery	2	9	4
5	Mike Channon	1	11	3
50 metres Swim				
1	Tony Greig	10	17.50	2
2	J. H. Stracey	7	12	5
3	David Hemery	4	13	4
4	Chay Blyth	2	8.50	7
5	John Conteh	1	18	1

Rowing (100 metres, single skiffs)

1	Chay Blyth	10	19.50	=4
2	David Hemery	7	20	3
3	Colin Bell	4	23	2
4	Tony Greig	2	19.50	=4
5	Mike Channon	1	15	7

N.B. Blyth allowed to compete by the adjudicators as rowing is not his speciality. (His sport is sailing).

Football penalties (5 attempts from the penalty spot. Goalkeeper Peter Shilton, England)

1	Tony Greig (5 goals)		10	29.50	2
2 ⎰	John Conteh (2 goals)	4.33	32.33		1
	David Hemery (2 goals)	4.33	24.33		3
⎱	J. H. Stracey (2 goals)	4.33	23.33		4
5	Chay Blyth (1 goal)		1	20.50	6

Cycle race (400 metres, time trials)

1	John Conteh (37.6 secs)	10	42.33	1
2	David Hemery (38.3 secs)	7	31.33	2
3	Colin Bell (39.1 secs)	4	27	4
4	Mike Channon (39.2 secs)	2	17	7
5	Tony Greig (39.6 secs)	1	30.50	3

Gymnasium tests (parallel bars dips, standing vertical jumps, 1 minute squat thrusts)

1	John Conteh	8.50	50.83	1
	David Hemery	8.50	39.83	2
3	Colin Bell	4	31	4
4	Chay Blyth	2	22.50	6
5	Tony Greig	1	31.50	3

Cricket tournament
(automatic bowling machine, 11 fielders, 6 ball over)

1	John Conteh (6 runs)	10	28	1
2	J. H. Stracey (5 runs)	7	19	=2
3 ⎰	Colin Bell (3 runs)	3	19	=2
⎱	Mike Channon (3 runs)	3	14	5
5	Chay Blyth (2 runs)	1	9.50	7

600 metres Steeplechase
(Hemery on handicap)

1	Colin Bell	10	41	3
2	John Conteh	7	57.83	1
3	Mike Channon	4	21	7
4	David Hemery	2	41.83	2
5	J. H. Stracey	1	24.33	5

EUROPEAN SUPERSTARS 1975 – BRITISH HEAT

Note: No UK championship held this year.

Five heats of the European competition held during the summer and autumn throughout Europe, followed by the first-ever European final, which was staged in Rotterdam, Holland.

Competitors

Belgium: Jackie Ickx (Motor racing: twice winner Le Mans)
Italy: Nicola Pietrangeli (Lawn Tennis: ex-world No.1 hard court player)
Holland: Ties Kruize (Hockey: 1972 Olympic goal scoring record holder)
France: Jean-Claude Bouttier (Boxing: former European champion)
Spain: Carlos Rexach (Football: international captain)
Sweden: Bjorn Nordqvist (Football: World Cup captain)
Great Britain: Colin Bell (Football: Manchester City and England)
David Hemery (Athletics: Olympic gold medallist, 1973 UK Superstars champion)

Points system: As for UK championships.

Prize money: Each heat: Winner £2,500, 2nd £1,500, 3rd £1,000, 4th £750.

1 Ties Kruize (Holl)	56 points	
×2 David Hemery (GB)	51½ points	
3 Colin Bell (GB)	37 points	
4 Jackie Ickx (Bel)	31 points	
5 Bjorn Nordqvist (Swe)	30 points	
6 Nicola Pietrangeli (I)	17 points	
7 Carlos Rexach (Sp)	14 points	
8 Jean-Claude Bouttier (F)	1½ points	

×Later competed in final (see finals results for details of qualification etc)

100 metres (Seconds)
1 Kruize (Holl)   12.1
2 Bell (GB)   12.2
3 Rexach (Sp)   12.5
4 Nordqvist (Swe)   12.5
5 Ickx (Bel)   13.0
6 Pietrangeli (I)   13.9
7 Bouttier (F)   14.0

†Hemery

N.B.:

†Barred under speciality rule

*Opted out under 8 out of 10 events rule

150 metres Single Skiff Rowing
1 Hemery (GB)   50.0
2 Nordqvist (Swe)   50.2
3 Kruize (Holl)   53.0
4 Bell (GB)   54.5
5 Ickx (Bel)   1:01.8
6 Pietrangeli (I)   1:02.2
7 Rexach (Sp)   1:03.6
8 Bouttier (F)   1:06.0

Gym tests

Medicine Ball throw
Pietrangeli   9m 50
Bell   9m 49
Hemery   9m 32
Nordqvist   9m 04
Rexach   8m 88
Ickx   8m 36
Bouttier   8m 20

Parallel Bars dips
Hemery   26
Ickx   24
Bell   19
Nordqvist   19
Rexach   9
Bouttier   8
Pietrangeli   4

Squat Thrusts (in one minute)
Hemery   71
Ickx   57
Nordqvist   55
Bell   51
Bouttier   50
Pietrangeli   43
Rexach   36

Overall placing for gym tests
(each test: 1st 7 points, 2nd 6 points etc)
1 Hemery (GB)
2 Bell (GB)   14.5
3 Ickx (Bel)   14
4 Nordqvist (Swe)   13.5
5 Pietrangeli (I)   10
6 Rexach (Sp)   7
7 Bouttier (F)   6
*Kruize

Weightlifting (decided on O'Carroll Formula of strength against body weight)

		Body weight	Actual weight lifted	O'Carroll converted weight lifted
1	Hemery (GB)	72.8 k	87.5 k	89.33 k
2	Nordqvist (Swe)	73.8 k	80.0 k	81.04 k
3	Kruize (Holl)	84.5 k	85.0 k	79.22 k
4	Ickx (Bel)	69.0 k	65.0 k	68.64 k
5	Bell (GB)	71.8 k	65.0 k	66.88 k
6 {	Bouttier (F)	76.0 k	60.0 k	59.64 k
}	Rexach (Sp)	76.2 k	60.0 k	59.64 k
8	Pietrangeli (I)	88.6 k	55.0 k	49.94 k

Soccer penalties (goalkeeper Ray Clemence of Liverpool and England)

Five attempts
1 Pietrangeli (I)   4
  (decided after play-off)
2 Kruize (Holl)   4
3 Ickx (Bel)   2
4 { Hemery (GB)   1
  { Bouttier (F)   1
†Bell, Rexach and Nordqvist

800 metre Cycling (Time trials to qualify for match-race finals)

Qualifiers
1 Ickx   1 min. 15.4 secs
2 Hemery   1 m 16.0 secs
3 Kruize   1 m 16.6 secs
4 Nordqvist   1 m 17.9 secs

Match races:
Hemery beat Ickx
Kruize beat Nordqvist

Overall placings
1 Hemery (GB)
2 Ickx (Bel)
3 Kruize (Holl)
4 Nordqvist (Swe)
5 Rexach (Sp)   1 m 18.7 secs
6 Bell (GB)   1 m 19.0 secs
7 Bouttier (F)   1 m 23.4 secs
8 Pietrangeli (I)   1 m 25.6 secs

600 metres Steeplechase

(Hemery 100 metre handicap as event near to speciality)
1 Bell (GB)   1 m 36.2 secs
2 Kruize (Holl)   1 m 40.1 secs
3 Nordqvist (Swe)   1 m 46.4 secs
4 Ickx (Bel)   1 m 52.0 secs
5 Rexach (Sp)   1 m 52.1 secs
6 Hemery (GB)   1 m 52.2 secs (fell)
  Bouttier (F) did not finish

*Pietrangeli

Swimming

(66 2/3 yards (60.66 metres) Freestyle
1 Kruize (Holl)   42.7
2 Hemery (GB)   43.3
3 Pietrangeli (I)   54.6
4 Nordqvist (Swe)   63.9

* Ickx, Bouttier, Bell, Rexach

Pistol Shooting (at 15 metre range, .22 automatics, ISU silhouette targets. 10 shots, maximum score 100.

1 Ickx (Bel)   91
2 Bell (GB)   91
3 Nordqvist (Swe)   90
4 Pietrangeli (I)   90
5 Rexach (Sp)   88
6 Bouttier (F)   84

* Kruize, Hemery

Shoot-off
Ickx   10   10   10   10   10 (5 bulls)   50
Bell   9   9   9   8   7   42
Placings of Nordqvist and Pietrangeli decided on greater number of bulls scored.

Lawn Tennis (first player to reach 15 points and 2 points clear)

Semi-finals
Kruize beat Bell 15-10
Rexach beat Hemery 15-4
Final
Kruize beat Rexach 15-13
Overall Tennis placings
1 Kruize (Holl)
2 Rexach (Sp)
3 { Hemery (GB)
  { Bell (GB)

† Pietrangeli
*Ickx, Bouttier, Nordqvist

SWEDISH HEAT
Competitors
Great Britain: Malcolm Macdonald (Football: Newcastle United and England)
Holland: Harm Kuipers (Speed Skating: world champion)
Italy: Giacomo Agostini (Motor-cycling: world title holder)
Germany: Jochen Mass (Motor racing: Germany's No. 1 Grand Prix driver)
Belgium: Willi Steveniers (Basketball: Leading European player)
Spain: Angel Nieto (Motor-cycling: six times world champion)
Sweden: Kjell Johansson (Table Tennis: three times World Doubles champion)
Sweden: Anders Garderud (Athletics: world record holder 3,000 metre Steeplechase)

Final result
x1	Malcolm Macdonald (GB)	48 points
x2 {	Harm Kuipers (Holl)	45 points
	Jochen Mass (Ger)	45 points
4	Kjell Johansson (Swe)	35 points
5	Willi Steveniers (Bel)	22 points
6	Giacomo Agostini (I)	20 points
7	Anders Garderud (Swe)	16 points
8	Angel Nieto (Sp)	8 points

100 metres
1	Macdonald (GB)	10.9 secs
2	Johansson (Swe)	11.6 secs
3	Kuipers (Holl)	12.2 secs
4	Garderud (Swe)	12.4 secs
5	Steveniers (Bel)	12.5 secs
6	Agostini (I)	12.8 secs
7	Nieto (Sp)	15.0 secs

*Mass

150 metres Rowing
1	Agostini (I)	50.5
2	Mass (Ger)	55.5
3	Steveniers (Bel)	1:09.0
4	Kuipers (Holl)	1:17.2
5	Garderud (Swe)	1:19.8
6	Johansson (Swe)	1:22.2
7	Macdonald (GB)	1:23.5
8	Nieto (Sp)	1:42.9

Soccer penalties (goalkeeper Goran Hagberg (Oster and Sweden).
5 attempts
1	Steveniers (Bel)	4 goals
2	Nieto (Sp)	2 goals

(play-off for 3rd, 4th and 5th places after triple tie of 1 goal each)
3 Garderud (Swe)
4 Johansson (Swe)
5 Agostini (I)
6 Mass (Ger)

†Macdonald
*Kuipers

Pistol Shooting (9mm army pistol (M40), 15 metres range, 10 shots, maximum score 100)
1	Macdonald (GB)	93
2	Kuipers (Holl)	76
3	Agostini (I)	74
4	Mass (Ger)	70
5	Nieto (Sp)	67
6	Johansson (Swe)	60
7	Steveniers (Bel)	54
8	Garderud (Swe)	38

800 metres Cycling (time trials to qualifiers for match-race finals)
1	Kuipers	1:10.2
2	Mass	1:12.2
3	Johansson	1:13.9
4	Steveniers	1:16.2

Match-race results
Kuipers beat Mass
Johansson beat Steveniers

Overall placings
1	Kuipers (Holl)	
2	Mass (Ger)	
3	Johansson (Swe)	
4	Steveniers (Bel)	
5	Agostini (I)	1:17.3
6	Macdonald (GB)	1:17.5
7	Nieto (Sp)	1:18.0
8	Garderud (Swe)	1:29.5

Weightlifting

	Body weight	Actual weight lifted	O'Carroll converted weight lifted
1 Macdonald (GB)	83.0 k	92.5 k	87.32 k
2 Mass (Ger)	76.1 k	85.0 k	84.15 k
3 Kuipers (Holl)	86.7 k	77.5 k	71.61 k
4 Steveniers (Bel)	74.5 k	70.0 k	70.35 k
5 Agostini (I)	68.8 k	65.0 k	68.97 k
6 Nieto (Sp)	57.5 k	no lift	—

*Johansson, Garderud

Gym tests
Medicine Ball throw
Macdonald (GB)	11.11m
Mass (Ger)	10.04m
Agostini (I)	8.49m
Kuipers (Holl)	7.64m
Garderud (Swe)	7.41m
Nieto (Sp)	5.90m

Parallel Bars dips
Mass	31
Kuipers	25
Agostini	24
Macdonald	14
Nieto	13
Garderud	8

Squat Thrusts (in one minute)
Macdonald	71
Kuipers	71
Mass	69
Agostini	66
Garderud	64
Nieto	56

Overall placings
(each test: 1st 7 points, 2nd 6 points etc)
1 Mass (Ger)	15
2 Macdonald (GB)	14½
3 Kuipers (Holl)	13½
4 Agostini (I)	11
5 Garderud (Swe)	5
6 Nieto (Sp)	4

*Johansson, Steveniers

50 metres Swimming
1 Mass (Ger)	30.5
2 Kuipers (Holl)	37.5
3 Garderud (Swe)	37.5
4 Johansson (Swe)	39.2
5 Steveniers (Bel)	44.5

*Macdonald, Agostini, Nieto

Lawn Tennis
Semi-finals
Macdonald beat Garderud 18-16
Johansson beat Mass 15-5
Final
Johansson beat Macdonald 15-6
Play-off for 3rd and 4th place
Garderud beat Mass 15-13

Overall tennis placings
1 Johnasson (Swe)
2 Macdonald (GB)
3 Garderud (Swe)
4 Mass (Ger)

*Kuipers, Agostini, Steveniers, Nieto

600 metres Steeplechase
1 Johansson (Swe)	1:41.0
2 Kuipers (Holl)	1:46.7
3 Macdonald (GB)	1:52.5
4 Steveniers (Bel)	2:08.8
5 Agostini (I)	2:14.5
6 Nieto (Sp)	2:19.8

†Garderud
*Mass

DUTCH HEAT

Great Britain: James Hunt (Motor racing: No. 1 Grand Prix driver, later to become world champion)

Belgium: Jeff Jurion (Football: former international captain and European Cup player from Anderlecht)

Germany: Hendrik Snoek (Show Jumping: world championship team member, British Derby winner)

Spain: Perico Fernandez (Boxing: winner of European and World Light Welterweight titles)

Sweden: Borje Salming (Ice Hockey: one-million dollar contract player with Toronto Maple Leafs in Canada)

Switzerland: Emerson Fittipaldi (Motor racing: world champion)

Holland: Gijs Van Lennep (Motor racing: winner of Le Mans European 5000 and Targa Florida)

Ard Schenk (Speed Skating: three Olympic gold medals and Olympic record holder)

Final result

×1	Ard Schenk (Holl)	47 points
2	Borje Salming (Swe)	45 points
3	James Hunt (GB)	38 points
4	Hendrik Snoek (Ger)	31 points
5	Gijs Van Lennep (Holl)	23 points
6	Jeff Jurion (Bel)	21 points
7	Perico Fernandez (Sp)	19 points
8	Emerson Fittipaldi (Sz)	15 points

100 metres

1	Jurion (Bel)	12.1
2	Salming (Swe)	12.1
3	Snoek (Ger)	12.1
4	Schenk (Holl)	12.2
5	Fernandez (Sp)	12.7
6	Hunt (GB)	13.0
7	Fittipaldi (Sz)	13.1
8	Van Lennep (Holl)	14.4

150 metres Rowing

1	Van Lennep (Holl)	50.4
2	Hunt (GB)	57.2
3	Fittipaldi (Sz)	1:02.8
4	Jurion (Bel)	1:12.0
5	Schenk (Holl)	1:21.8
6	Salming (Swe)	1:50.5

*Snoek, Fernandez

Gym tests

Medicine Ball throw

Jurion	9.05m
Fernandez	8.82m
Snoek	8.06m
Fittipaldi	7.54m
Van Lennep	7.13m

Parallel Bars dips

Van Lennep	24
Fernandez	23
Snoek	20
Fittipaldi	20
Jurion	16

Squat Thrusts (1 minute)

Fernandez	67
Van Lennep	65
Snoek	61
Jurion	60
Fittipaldi	59

Final placings

1	Fernandez (Sp)
2	Van Lennep (Holl)
3	Snoek (Ger)
4	Jurion (Bel)
5	Fittipaldi (Sz)

*Salming, Hunt, Schenk

Weightlifting

	Body weight	Actual weight lifted	O'Carroll converted weight lifted
1 Salming (Sw)	83.0 k	95.0 k	89.40 k
2 Schenk (Holl)	97.0 k	90.0 k	77.76 k
3 Jurion (Bel)	75.0 k	65.0 k	65.07 k
4 Hunt	76.5 k	60.0 k	59.16 k

*Snoek, Fittipaldi, Fernandez, Van Lennep

800 metres Cycling (The first two riders in each heat qualified for the final. The three remaining raced-off for 5th place)

Heat 1

1 Fittipaldi (Sz)	1:56.0
2 Snoek (Ger)	1:57.4
3 Fernandez (Sp)	1:58.8

Heat 2

1 Schenk (Ger)	1:49.8
2 Hunt (GB)	1:52.6
3 Van Lennep (Holl)	1:52.8
4 Jurion (Bel)	2:01.0

Race for 5th place

1 Van Lennep	2:08.2
2 Jurion	2:08.4
3 Fernandez	2:12.5

Final

1 Schenk	1:49.9
2 Fittipaldi	1:51.8
3 Hunt	1:52.3
4 Snoek	1:54.3

*Salming

Lawn Tennis

1st round

Snoek (Ger) beat Jurion (Bel) 17-15
Hunt (GB) beat Fittipaldi (Sz) 15-1
Van Lennep (Holl) bt Schenk (Holl)
15-12
Salming (Swe) bt Fernandez (Sp) 15-5

Semi-finals

Salming beat Snoek 15-10
Hunt beat Van Lennep 15-2

3rd and 4th place play-off

Snoek beat Van Lennep 15-9

Final

Hunt beat Salming 15-6

Overall placings

1 Hunt
2 Salming
3 Snoek
4 Van Lennep
5 Jurion
   (highest scoring 1st round loser)

Pistol Shooting (8 metres, air pistols)

1 Snoek (Ger)	5 hits	11 shots
2 Schenk (Holl)	5 hits	13 shots
3 Hunt (GB)	5 hits	13 shots
4 Fittipaldi (Sz)	5 hits	15 shots
5 Fernandez (Sp)	4 hits	19 shots
6 Salming (Sw)	3 hits	
7 Jurion (Bel)	3 hits	
8 Van Lennep (Holl)	1 hit	

(2nd and 3rd place and 6th and 7th places were decided on time)

50 metres Swimming

1 Salming (Swe)	32.6
2 Snoek (Ger)	36.2
3 Fernandez (Sp)	40.7
4 Van Lennep (Holl)	44.4
5 Fittipaldi (Sz)	50.2

*Hunt, Schenk, Jurion

Soccer penalties

(Goalkeeper Piet Schrijvers (Ajax and Holland). 5 attempts

1 Schenk (Holl)	5
2 Hunt (GB)	4
3 Salming (Swe)	2
4 Fernandez (Sp)	1
5 Van Lennep (Holl)	1
6 Snoek (Ger)	1
7 Fittipaldi (Sz)	0

(4th, 5th and 6th place decided after a play-off)

†Jurion

600 metres Steeplechase

1 Schenk (Holl)	1:44.1
2 Salming (Swe)	1:47.2
3 Hunt (GB)	1:50.2
4 Jurion (Bel)	1:54.9
5 Fernandez (Sp)	2:03.2

(Snoek (Ger) fell at the water jump on the first lap and retired injured)

*Van Lennep, Fittipaldi

BELGIAN HEAT

Competitors

Great Britain: Alan Pascoe (Athletics: Olympic silver medal hurdles, European and Commonwealth gold)

Spain: Jody Scheckter (Motor racing: British, Swedish and South African Grand Prix winner. South African born, Spanish resident)

Jose Duran (Boxing: national champion and world championship contender)

Holland: Joep Zoetemelk (Cycling: twice runner-up in Tour de France)

Sweden: Ricky Bruch (Athletics: Olympic and European medal winning discus thrower)

France: Guy Drut (Athletics: Olympic silver medal in Munich, 110 metre hurdles. Went on to win gold in Montreal)

Belgium: Freddie Maertens (Cycling: runner-up World Road race championships)

Paul Van Himst (Football: international captain)

Final result

ˣ1	Drut (F)	45	points
2	Van Himst (Bel)	41	points
3	Alan Pascoe (GB)	39½	points
4	Jody Scheckter (Sp)	38	points
5	Ricky Bruch (Swe)	33½	points
6	Joep Zoetemelk (Holl)	15	points
7	Jose Duran (Sp)	14	points
8	Freddie Maertens (Bel)	13	points

Gym tests

Medicine Ball throw

Bruch	19.73m
Drut	12.50m
Pascoe	10.33m
Scheckter	10.16m
Duran	8.61m
Maertens	8.09m

Parallel Bars dips

Scheckter	32
Bruch	25
Pascoe	22
Drut	21
Duran	9
Maertens	4

Squat Thrusts (1 minute)

Scheckter	79
Maertens	71
Pascoe	68
Drut	63
Duran	52
Bruch	51

Final placings

1 Scheckter (Sp)
2 Bruch (Swe)
3 Pascoe (GB)
4 Drut (F)
5 Maertens (Bel)
6 Duran (Sp)

*Zoetemelk, Van Himst

Lawn Tennis

1st round

Duran beat Pascoe	15-4
Van Himst beat Zoetemelk	15-0
Drut beat Maertens	15-8
Bruch beat Scheckter	18-16

Semi-finals

Drut beat Van Himst	15-10
Bruch beat Duran	15-9

3rd and 4th place play-off

Duran beat Van Himst	15-3

Final

Bruch beat Drut	15-8

Overall placings

1 Bruch (Swe)
2 Drut (F)
3 Duran (Sp)
4 Van Himst (Bel)
5 Scheckter (Sp) Highest scoring first round loser

150 metres Rowing

1	Drut (F)	1:18.2
2	Pascoe (GB)	1:49.0
3	Zoetemelk (Holl)	2:15.6
4	Maertens (Bel)	2:52.0
5	Van Himst (Bel)	4:23.6
6	Duran (Sp)	5:09.2

*Scheckter, Bruch

Pistol Shooting (.22 automatics, range 15 metres, 10 shots, maximum score 100)

1	Pascoe (GB)	79
2	Zoetemelk (Holl)	71
3	Van Himst (Bel)	69
4	Bruch (Swe)	66
5	Maertens (Bel)	60
6	Scheckter (Sp)	56
7	Drut (F)	35

*Duran

Weightlifting

	Body weight	Actual weight lifted	O'Carroll converted weight lifted
1 Bruch (Swe)	127.00 k	135.00 k	102.20 k
2 Drut (F)	78.00 k	102.50 k	100.04 k
3 Scheckter (Sp)	73.00 k	87.50 k	88.99 k
4 Pascoe (GB)	79.00 k	80.00 k	77.52 k
5 Maertens (Bel)	70.00 k	55.00 k	57.59 k
6 Van Himst (Bel)	81.50 k	60.00 k	57.00 k
7 Zoetemelk (Holl)	66.00 k	45.00 k	48.87 k

*Duran

800 metres Cycling
1st heat
1 Drut	1:25.49
2 Bruch	1:39.3

2nd Heat
1 Van Himst	1:25.25
2 Scheckter	1:25.8

3rd Heat
1 Pascoe	1:31.36
2 Duran	1:37.2

3rd and 4th place ride-off
1 Pascoe (visual decision)	1:35.30
2 Scheckter	1:35.30

1st and 2nd place ride-off
1 Van Himst	1:31.9
2 Drut	1:32.0

Final cycle race placings
1 Van Himst (Bel)
2 Drut (F)
3 Pascoe (GB)
4 Scheckter (Sp)
5 Duran (Sp)
6 Van Himst (Bel)
†Maertens, Zoetemelk

100 metres
1 Van Himst (Bel)	12.8
2 Scheckter (Sp)	13.1
3 Bruch (Swe)	13.2
4 Duran (Sp)	14.0
5 Maertens (Bel)	15.1
6 Zoetemelk (Holl)	16.1

†Pascoe, Drut

Soccer penalties
(Goalkeeper Christian Piot (Standard Liège and Belgium).

1 Drut (F)	4
2 Maertens (Bel)	3
3 Pascoe (GB)	3
4 Zoetemelk (Holl)	3
5 Bruch (Swe)	2
6 Duran (Sp)	0

2nd, 3rd and 4th places decided after play-off

†Van Himst
*Scheckter

600 metres Steeplechase
1 Van Himst (Bel)	2:02.8
2 Duran (Sp)	2:03.9
3 Scheckter (Sp)	2:08.1
4 Zoetemelk (Holl)	2:20.2

†Pascoe, Drut
*Bruch, Maertens

50 metres Swimming
1 Scheckter (Sp)	30.0
2 Pascoe (GB)	35.0
3 Van Himst (Bel)	40.2
4 Drut (F)	42.6
5 Bruch (Swe)	44.3
6 Duran (Sp)	51.2
7 Maertens (Bel)	51.3
8 Zoetemelk (Holl)	59.6

SPANISH HEAT

Great Britain: Jonah Barrington (Squash: former British Amateur and British Open champion)

France: Jean-Claude Killy (Ski-ing: triple Olympic champion and double world champion)

Jean-Pierre Danguillaume (Cycling: bronze medal World Road race championships)

Belgium: Fons Brijdenbach (Athletics: national 100, 200 and 400 metres champion, European indoor title holder)

Sweden: Kjell Isaksson (Athletics: three times world pole vault record holder)

Holland: Tom Okker (Lawn Tennis: Dutch all time No. 1)

Spain: Angel Gallardo (Golf: Portuguese, Spanish and Mexican Open winner)

Mariano Haro (Athletics: Olympic 10,000 metre runner)

Final Result

×1	Kjell Isaksson (Swe)	69 points
×2	Fons Brijdenbach (Bel)	41 points
3	Jean-Claude Killy (F)	39 points
4	Tom Okker (Holl)	29 points
×5	Mariano Haro (Sp)	21½ points
6	J-P Danguillaume (F)	17½ points
7	Angel Gallardo (Sp)	4 points

Note: Jonah Barrington (GB) withdrew after first day following dispute over gymnasium results.

100 metres

1	Isaksson (Swe)	12.1
2	Killy (F)	12.3
3	Okker (Holl)	12.8
4	Haro (Sp)	13.9
5	Danguillaume (F)	14.2
6	Gallardo (Sp)	15.0

† Brijdenbach
*Barrington

Pistol Shooting (semi-automatic .38s, range 15 metres, 10 shots, maximum score 100)

1	Isaksson (Swe)	92
2	Danguillaume (F)	84
3	Brijdenbach (Bel)	77
4	Gallardo (Sp)	75
5	Killy (F)	65
6	Barrington (GB)	49
7	Okker (Holl)	28
	Haro (Sp)	28

60.66 metres Swimming

1	Isaksson (Swe)	46.9
2	Okker (Holl)	48.5
3	Brijdenbach (Bel)	57.0
4	Danguillaume (F)	1:27.0

*Barrington, Killy, Haro, Gallardo

150 metres Rowing

1st Heat

Isaksson (Swe)	0:53.3
Danguillaume (F)	1:03.8
Brijdenbach (Bel)	1:10.1

2nd Heat

Killy (F)	0:54.2
Okker (Holl)	0:57.2
Gallardo (Sp)	1:14.3

Final

(First run stopped due to collision between Killy and Isaksson)

1	Killy	0:53.2
2	Isaksson	0:55.0
3	Okker	0:56.9
4	Danguillaume	1:03.1

5th place awarded to Brijdenbach as fastest non-final qualifier

Barrington (Absent from competition)
*Haro

Weightlifting

	Body weight	Actual weight lifted	O'Carroll converted weight lifted
1 Isaksson (Swe)	70.5 k	85.0 k	88.57 k
2 Barrington (GB)	68.0 k	75.0 k	79.95 k
3 Brijdenbach (Bel)	76.4 k	70.0 k	69.30 k
4 Killy (F)	71.7 k	60.0 k	61.74 k
5 Gallardo (Sp)	67.2 k	95.0 k	48.42 k
6 Haro (Sp)	57.6 k	40.0 k	48.36 k
7 Danguillaume (F)	71.0 k	45.0 k	46.53 k

*Okker

Gym tests
Medicine Ball Throw
Brijdenbach	9.65 m
Isaksson	9.51 m
Okker	7.92 m
Danguillaume	7.91 m
Barrington	6.85 m
Haro	5.41 m
Gallardo	5.12 m

Parallel Bars Dips
Isaksson	27
Barrington	25
Brijdenbach	18
Haro	11
Danguillaume	10
Gallardo	6
Okker	4

Squat Thrusts (1 minute)
Isaksson	61
Okker	56
Haro	52
Danguillaume	51
Brijdenbach	49
Gallardo	30
Barrington	25

(Disputed by Barrington)

Final results
1 Isaksson (Swe)
2 Brijdenbach (bel)
3 Okker (Holl)
4 Danguillaume (F)
5 Haro (Sp)
6 Barrington (GB)
7 Gallardo (sp)

*Killy

800 metres Cycling
1st Heat
Isaksson (Swe)	1:19.6
Brijdenbach (Bel)	1:19.9

2nd Heat
Killy (F)	1:13.2
Okker (Holl)	1:26.0

3rd Heat
Haro (Sp)	1:18.1
Gallardo (Sp)	1:28.0

1st, 2nd place ride-off
Killy	1:32.6
Haro	1:34.0

3rd, 4th place ride-off
Brijdenbach	3:02.7
Isaksson	3:03.5

Final cycle placings
1 Killy
2 Haro
3 Brijdenbach
4 Isaksson
5 Okker
6 Gallardo

Barrington absent
†Danguillaume

Soccer penalties (Goalkeeper Pat Jennings (Tottenham Hotspur and Northern Ireland). 5 attempts)
1 Brijdenbach (Bel)	4
2 Okker (Holl)	3
3 Killy (F)	3
4 Haro (Sp)	1
5 Gallardo (Sp)	0
6 Danguillaume (F)	0

(2nd and 3rd places and 5th and 6th places were decided by a kick-off)
Barrington absent
*Isaksson

Lawn Tennis
Bye: Barrington and Haro
1st round

Danguillaume beat Gallardo	15-6
Brijdenbach beat Killy	15-7

Semi-finals

Barrington beat Danguillaume	15-2
Brijdenbach beat Haro	15-1

3rd and 4th place play-off

Danguillaume beat Haro	15-7

Final

Barrington beat Brijdenbach	15-8

Overall tennis placings
1 Barrington (GB)
2 Brijdenbach (Bel)
3 Danguillaume (F)
4 Haro (Sp)
5 Killy (F) Highest scoring first round loser
6 Gallardo (Sp)

† Okker
*Isaksson

600 metres Steeplechase

1 Isaksson (Swe)	1:43.0
2 Haro (Sp)	1:45.8
3 Killy (F)	2:06.7
4 Okker (Holl)	2:08.6

(Haro 40 metre handicap as he is an international athlete)

*Brijdenbach
*Gallardo, Danguillaume, Barrington absent

1975 EUROPEAN SUPERSTARS FINAL

Competitors
Great Britain: David Hemery (Athletics)
Malcolm Macdonald (Football)
France: Guy Drut (Athletics)
Germany: Jochen Mass (Motor racing)
Holland: Ard Schenk and Harm Kuipers (Speed Skating)
Sweden: Kjell Isaksson (Athletics)
Spain: Mariano Haro (Athletics)
Belgium: Fons Brijdenbach (Athletics)

Final result

1 Isaksson (Swe)	56 points	£5,000
2 Hemery (GB)	39 points	£3,000
3 Schenk (Holl)	36 points	£2,000
4 Mass (Ger)	30 points	£1,500
5 Brijdenbach (Bel)	21 points	
6 Kuipers (Holl)	20 points	
7 MacDonald (GB)	18.50 points	
8 Drut (F)	16.50 points	
9 Haro (Sp)	3 points	

Qualification for final
(a) Heat winners (Isaksson, Schenk, MacDonald, Drut, Kruize)
(b) Ties Kruize, winner of the British heat was unable to accept his place due to injuries received in a motor accident (see page 28). David Hemery was the next highest points scorer in that heat and was admitted to the final.
(c) The host nation, Holland, 2 competitors (Schenk and Kuipers)
(d) The non-regular competing nations (Germany, Switzerland, Italy and Spain) 2 competitors overall (Mass and Haro).

Note: Although Jody Scheckter represented Spain in the Belgian heat and scored 38 points, making him second to Jochen Mass of the non-regular nations, Scheckter was unable to accept his place due to outstanding engagements and Haro of Spain was admitted as the next highest scorer.

100 metres

1 MacDonald (GB)	10.7
2 Hemery (GB)	11.2
3 Isaksson (Swe)	11.5
4 Schenk (Holl)	11.6
5 Kuipers (Holl)	11.7
6 Haro (Sp)	13.2

N.B. Hemery and Isaksson 4 metres handicap as both competing in event near speciality.
*Brijdenbach, Drut, Mass

800 metres Cycling pursuit
1st Heat

1 Hemery (GB)	1:06.43
2 Haro (Sp)	1:08.72

2nd Heat

1 Kuipers (Holl)	1:01.82
2 Brijdenbach (Bel)	1:09.31

3rd Heat

1 Drut (F)	1:07.78
2 Mass (Ger)	1:09.17

4th Heat

1 Schenk (Holl)	1:03.93
2 MacDonald (GB)	1:10.26

3rd, 4th place final

3 Hemery	1:13.47
4 Drut	1:17.03

1st, 2nd place final

1 Kuipers	1:03.42
2 Schenk	1:08.39

The point for 5th place went to Haro, as fastest non-qualifier

*Isaksson

Weightlifting	Body weight	Actual weight lifted	O'Carroll converted weight lifted
1 Isaksson (Swe)	69.7 k	97.5 k	102.47 k
2 Drut (F)	79.0 k	97.5 k	94.48 k
3 Hemery (GB)	73.8 k	92.5 k	93.70 k
4 Macdonald (GB)	84.5 k	95.0 k	88.54 k
5 Mass (Ger)	77.0 k	82.5 k	81.09
6 Kuipers (Holl)	87.0 k	80.0 k	73.28 k
7 Haro (Sp)	59.3 k	47.5 k	56.34 k

Gymnasium tests
Medicine Ball Throw
MacDonald (GB)	12.48 m
Drut (F)	12.30 m
Isaksson (Swe)	10.96 m
Schenk (Holl)	10.87 m
Brijdenbach (Bel)	10.78 m
Mass (Ger)	9.74 m
Hemery (GB)	9.11 m
Kuipers (Holl)	8.80 m
Haro (Sp)	5.96 m

Parallel Bars Dips
Hemery	37
Isaksson	36
Mass	33
Drut	28
Kuipers	26
Brijdenbach	23
Haro	17
MacDonald	15
Schenk	11

Squat Thrusts
Hemery	78
Isaksson	69
Mass	68
MacDonald	66
Schenk	59
Kuipers	58
Drut	55
Brijdenbach	54
Haro	44

Overall placings
1 Isaksson
2 Hemery
3 Mass
4 Drut
  MacDonald
6 Schenk
7 {Kuipers
   {Brijdenbach
9 Haro

150 metres Rowing
1st Heat
1	Isaksson (Swe)	46.3
2	Mass (Ger)	51.2
3	Kuipers (Holl)	59.7
4	Brijdenbach (Bel)	1:22.6

2nd Heat
1	Schenk (Holl)	55.2
2	Hemery (GB)	58.5
3	Drut (F)	58.7

Macdonald (GB did not finish)
Final
(2 heat winners and 2 fastest losers)
1	Isaksson	43.7
2	Schenk	50.1
3	Mass	52.3
4	Hemery	69.9

5th place (fastest non-qualifier) Drut

*Haro

Lawn Tennis
1st round
Hemery beat Drut	15-10
Isaksson beat Haro	15-6
Mass beat Macdonald	15-13
Brijdenbach beat Schenk	15-4

Semi-finals
Brijdenbach beat Hemery	15-8
Isaksson beat Mass	15-13

3rd, 4th place play-off
Hemery beat Mass	15-11

Final
Brijdenbach beat Isaksson	15-11

Final tennis placings
1 Brijdenbach (bel)
2 Isaksson (Swe)
3 Hemery (GB)
4 Mass (Ger)
5 Macdonald (GB)
    Highest scoring first round loser

*Kuipers

Pistol Shooting

Range: 8 metres. Weapons: Air Pistols. Time limit: 5 minutes. Target: 5 × 2 inch-diameter clay discs.

	hits	shots	time	score
1 Schenk (holl)	5	14	4:55.83	73
2 Mass (Ger)	5	18	3:31.62	61
3 Macdonald (GB)	5	18	3:49.01	61
4 Brijdenbach (Holl)	3	20	4:00.15	33
5 Isaksson (Swe)	2	20	4:58.14	22
6 Kuipers (Holl)	1	20	4:23.98	11
7 Drut (F)	0	20	4:38.14	0
8 Harro (Sp)	0	20	4:55.83	0

*Hemery
*Brijdenbach, Schenk

Soccer penalties

(Goalkeeper Ilija Pantelic (Yugoslavia and Paris-St. Germain). 5 attempts.

Final placings

1 Schenk (Holl)	3
(kick-off to decide placing)	
2 Brijdenbach (Bel)	3
3 Drut (F)	1
4 Mass (Ger)	1
(kick-off to decide placing)	
5 Haro (Sp)	0

† Macdonald
*Hemery, Kuipers

50 metres Swimming

1 Mass (Ger)	30.2
2 Hemery (GB)	31.6
3 Isaksson (Swe)	35.2
4 Kuipers (Holl)	37.2
5 Drut (F)	39.4
6 Brijdenbach (Bel)	42.0

*Schenk, Macdonald, Haro

600 metres Steeplechase

1 Isaksson (Swe)	1:38.8
2 Kuipers (Holl)	1:40.3
3 Hemery (GB)	1:40.4
4 Brijdenbach (Bel)	1:44.3
5 Haro (Sp)	1:44.4
6 Macdonald (GB)	1:45.7
7 Schenk (Holl)	1:48.9

N.B. Hemery and Brijdenbach 40 metres handicap, Haro 15 metres (near to speciality rule)

*Drut, Mass

U.K. NATIONAL SUPERSTARS 1976

Competitors (10)
David Hemery (Athletics)
John Conteh (Boxing)
Malcolm Macdonald (Football)
Stan Bowles (Football)
James Hunt (Motor racing)
Jonah Barrington (Squash)
Gareth Edwards (Rugby Union)
David Duckham (Rugby Union)
J.P.R. Williams (Rugby Union)
David Starbrook (Judo)

Final result

1 Hemery	55½ points	£2,500
2 Conteh	29 points	£1,500
3 Hunt	28 points	£1,000
4 Edwards	24 points	£750
5 Duckham	23 points	
6 Starbrook	21½ points	
7 Barrington	18 points	
8 {Macdonald	16 points	
{Williams	16 points	
10 Bowles	7 points	

100 metres

1 MacDonald	11.0
2 Duckham	12.1
3 Starbrook	12.5
4 Bowles	12.6
5 Conteh	12.8
6 Hunt	13.0

*Barrington, Edwards, Hemery, Williams

125 metres Canoeing
1st Heat

1 Hemery	50.1
2 Starbrook	50.4
3 Duckham	52.2
4 Edwards	55.0
5 Barrington	66.4

2nd Heat

1 Conteh	55.0
2 Hunt	55.4
3 Williams	58.1
MacDonald } capsized	
Bowles }	

Final (2nd run)

1 Hemery	49.3
2 Conteh	52.0
3 Hunt	53.4
4 Starbrook	53.8

Note: Duckham was ruled to have impeded Hunt in 1st run of final and was disqualified and race re-run

500 metres Cycling
Time-trial Heats
1st Heat

Duckham	48.4
Edwards	50.1

2nd Heat

Williams	46.9
Bowles	48.8

3rd Heat

Hemery	45.4
Barrington	47.9

4th Heat

Hunt	45.7
Conteh	58.1

5th Heat

MacDonald	46.1
Starbrook	48.9

Conteh, whose pedal straps slipped, and Starbrook, who bent an axle on his cycle, were given a second time trial by the Overall Referee, (Maj. Michael Campbell-Lamerton)

6th Heat

Conteh	46.3
Starbrook	48.4

3rd, 4th place ride-off

1 Conteh	43.5
2 MacDonald	43.9

1st, 2nd place ride-off

1 Hemery	47.5
2 Hunt	47.6

Overall placings
1 Hemery
2 Hunt
3 Conteh
4 Macdonald
5 Williams (fastest non-qualifier)

Soccer skills (Slalom-Dribbling test, 3 runs, goalkeeper Ian Turner of Southampton)

	Goals	Time
1 Edwards	2	1:13.4
2 Barrington	2	1:17.0
3 Hunt	2	1:20.0
4 Conteh	2	1:20.8
5 Williams	1	1:12.5
6 Starbrook	1	1:16.0
7 Hemery	1	1:18.2
8 Duckham	0	1:20.2

†Macdonald, Bowles

Weightlifting (Amount lifted over body-weight)

		Body weight	Weight lifted	Score
1	Edwards	79.3 k	100.0 k	20.7 k
2	Hemery	73.9 k	92.5 k	18.6 k
3	Macdonald	83.4 k	97.5 k	14.1 k
4	Conteh	82.1 k	95.0 k	12.9 k
5	Williams	87.9 k	90.0 k	2.1 k
6	Duckham	90.7 k	92.5 k	1.8 k
7	Barrington	68.4 k	70.0 k	1.6 k
8	Starbrook	91.1 k	92.5 k	1.4 k
9	Bowles	72.5 k	65.0 k	− 7.5 k
10	Hunt	78.4 k	60.0 k	−18.4 k

Tennis

Bye
Edwards
1st round

Hunt beat Macdonald	15-3
Barrington beat Bowles	15-12
Williams beat Hemery	15-2

Semi-finals

Barrington beat Hunt	15-13
Williams beat Edwards	15-2

3rd, 4th place final

Hunt beat Edwards	15-11

1st, 2nd place final
Williams beat Barrington-15-4

Overall placings

1	Williams	3	Hunt
2	Barrington	4	Edwards

5 Bowles highest scoring non-qualifier)

Pistol Shooting (15 metre range, .38 calibre, 5 shots at I.S.U. target)
Four competitors (Hemery, Conteh, Duckham and Hunt) all shot a score of 46 out of a maximum of 50. This resulted in a shoot-off to decide the top four places as follows:

1 Hemery	49 (4 bulls and a 9)
2 Conteh	45 (2 bulls, 3 × 9, 1 × 8)
3 Duckham	43
	(2 bulls, 1 × 9, 1 × 8, 1 × 6)
4 Hunt	35
	(1 × 9, 1 × 8, 1 × 7, 1 × 6, 1 × 5)

Other placings from original shoot:

5	Edwards	42
6	Macdonald	41
	Williams	41
8	Starbrook	31
9	Barrington	29
10	Bowles	20

66 2/3 yards Swimming: 1 Hemery 42.0. 2 Starbrook 48.1. 3 Bowles 52.1. 4 Williams 52.2.
*Barrington, Conteh, Duckham, Edwards, Macdonald, Hunt

Gymnasium tests

Parallel Bar Dips

1	Starbrook	49
2	Hemery	38
3	Conteh	30
4	Edwards	27
	Duckham	27
6	Barrington	21
7	Macdonald	17
8	Williams	12

Squat Thrusts (1 minute)

1	Hemery	76
2	Starbrook	74
3	Williams	73
4	Duckham	71
5	Conteh	70
6	Macdonald	67
7	Barrington	66
8	Edwards	56

Overall result

1	Hemery
	Starbrook
3	Conteh
4	Duckham
5	Williams
6	Edwards
7	Barrington
	Macdonald

*Bowles, Hunt

600 metres Steeplechase

1	Duckham	1:40.8
2	Hunt	1:41.8
3	Barrington	1:41.9
4	Conteh	1:46.0
5	Edwards	1:46.8
6	Bowles	1:50.7
7	Macdonald	1:57.7

*Hemery, Starbrook, Williams

EUROPEAN SUPERSTARS 1976 — BRITISH HEAT

Prize money: Winner of heat $5,000, 2nd $3,000, 3rd $2,000, 4th $1,500.
Final: Winner and European Superstar $10,000, 2nd $6,000, 3rd $4,000, 4th $3,000.
For competitors who have amateur status, prize-money was paid to their sports associations as before.

Headings
Competitors
Great Britain: John Conteh (Boxing: World Light-Heavyweight champion, UK Superstar 1974)
       Peter Shilton (Football: goalkeeper, England and Stoke City)
Switzerland: Bernard Russi (Ski-ing: Olympic gold and silver medals)
Sweden: Thomas Magnusson (Ski-ing: World Cross Country champion)
France: Henri Duvillard (Ski-ing: world professional champion)
Holland: Piet Kleine (Speed Skating: world and Olympic champion)
Belgium: Maurice Maertens (Football: World Cup squad 1970)
Germany: Christian Neureuther (Ski-ing: national Slalom champion and World Cup medallist)

Final result
×1	Conteh (GB)	42.5 points
2	Duvillard (F)	36 points
3	Bernard Russi (Sz)	35 points
4	Neureuther (Ger)	31.5 points
5	Magnusson (Swe)	29.5 points
6	Shilton (GB)	27 points
7	Maertens (Bel)	19 points
8	Kleine (Holl)	16.5 points

100 metres
1	Russi (Sz)	11.5
2	Shilton (GB)	11.7
3	Neureuther (Ger)	11.8
4	Maertens (Bel)	12.3
5	Conteh (GB)	12.4
6	Magnusson (Swe)	13.8

*Duvillard, Kleine

50 metres Swimming
1	Magnusson (Swe)	34.5
2	Russi (Sz)	35.2
3	Maertens (Bel)	44.8
4	Kleine (Holl)	47.4
5	Shilton (GB)	
	(Non-qualifier from heats)	

*Conteh, Duvillard, Neureuther

600 metres Steeplechase
1	Shilton	1:39.9
2	Russi	1:40.9
3	Magnusson	1:41.0
4	Conteh	1:41.2
5	Maertens	1:45.3
6	Kleine	1:46.2
7 {	Duvillard	2:06.6
	Neureuther	2:06.6

Weightlifting	Body weight	Weight lifted	Score
1 Duvillard	70.1 k	85.0 k	14.9 k
2 Conteh	80.3 k	90.0 k	9.7 k
3 Kleine	80.3 k	60.0 k	-20.3 k

*Shilton, Russi, Magnusson, Maertens, Neureuther

Soccer skills
(Goalkeeper Phil Parkes (QPR and England)
Two-part competition (Slalom-dribbling and penalties)
Slalom (3 runs against the clock)

	Goals	Seconds	Points
1 Neureuther (Ger)	3	41.0	6
2 Duvillard (F)	2	42.4	5
3 Russi (Sz)	2	43.2	4
4 Conteh (GB)	1	36.0	3
5 Magnusson (Swe)	1	44.7	2
6 Kleine (Holl)	1	46.0	1

Penalties (5 attempts)
Neureuther scored 4, Magnusson and Russi 2 each, the others 1 each. This resulted in a sudden-death play-off to decide the penalty section with the following result:

1 Neureuther	6 points
2 Magnusson	5 points
3 Russi	4 points
4 Kleine	3 points
5 Duvillard	2 points
6 Conteh	1 point

Overall soccer skills placings

1	Neureuther	12 points
2	Russi	8 points
3	Duvillard	7 points
	Magnusson	7 points
5	Conteh	4 points
	Kleine	4 points

† Shilton, Maertens

Shooting (.38 FN Browning, 15 metres, 5 shot — maximum score 50)

1	Conteh (GB)	47
2	Shilton (GB)	45
3	Maertens (Bel)	40
4	Duvillard (F)	39
5	Magnusson (Swe)	35
	Neureuther (Ger)	35
7	Russi (Sz)	17
8	Kleine (Holl)	9

Gymnasium tests
Parallel Bars Dips

	Duvillard (F)	28
1	Conteh (GB)	28
4	Russi (Sz)	28
	Neureuther (Ger)	24
5	Maertens (Bel)	21
	Shilton (GB)	21

Squat Thrusts (1 minute)

1	Conteh	80
2	Neureuther	72
3	Duvillard	70
4	Shilton	69
	Russi	69
6	Maertens	59

Overall result

1	Conteh
2	Duvillard
3	Neureuther
4	Russi
5	Shilton
6	Maertens

*Kleine, Magnusson

125 metres Canoeing (touring single kayaks)
Qualifying times (Fastest four to final)

1	Conteh (GB)	38.8
2	Neureuther (Ger)	40.3
3	Duvillard (F)	41.2
4	Magnusson (Swe)	42.8
5	Shilton (GB)	43.8
6	Maertens (Bel)	44.7
7	Kleine (Holl)	51.6

Final placings

1	Conteh	40.3
2	Duvillard	41.2
3	Neureuther (Ger)	42.0
4	Magnusson (Swe)	42.5
5	Shilton (GB)	
	(fastest non-qualifier)	

*Russi

Table Tennis
1st round

Conteh beat Kleine	21-8
Neureuther beat Duvillard	21-12
Maertens beat Shilton	21-13
Magnusson beat Russi	21-15

Semi-finals

Neureuther beat Conteh	21-11
Magnusson beat Maertens	21-7

3rd, 4th place final

Maertens beat Conteh	22-20

1st, 2nd place final

Magnusson beat Neureuther	21-11

Final table tennis placings

1 Magnusson (Swe)
2 Neureuther (Ger)
3 Maertens (Bel)
4 Conteh (GB)
5 Russi (Sz)
    (Highest scoring 1st round loser)

460 metres Cycling
1st Heat

Duvillard (F)	41.5
Shilton (GB)	44.5

2nd Heat

Kleine (Holl)	41.0
Russi (Sz)	44:0

3rd Heat

Maertens (Bel)	42.6
Magnusson (Swe)	45.0

4th Heat

Neureuther (Ger)	42.9

1st, 2nd place final

1 Kleine	40.2
2 Duvillard	43.0

3rd, 4th place final

1 Maertens	42.8
2 Neureuther	42.9

Overall placings

1 Kleine
2 Duvillard
3 Maertens
4 Neureuther
5 Russi (fastest non-qualifier)

*Conteh

DUTCH HEAT

Great Britain: David Wilkie (Swimming: Olympic gold medal, world, European and Commonwealth champion)
France: Walter Spanghero (Ruby Union: 51 times an international)
Austria: Karl Schnabl (Ski Jumping: double Olympic medallist)
Denmark: Kresten Bjerre (Football: League appearance record holder)
Sweden: Anders Michanek (Speedway: 1974 world champion)
Belgium: Olin 'Corky' Bell (Basketball: ex-New York City Star, now top Belgian international)
Holland: Paul Litjens (Hockey: top Olympic goal scorer)
Wim Van Hanegem (Football: international and World Cup player from Feyenoord)

Final result

×1	Schnabl (Aus)	47 points
2	Michanek (Swe)	38 points
3 {	Litjens (Holl)	32 points
{×	Bell (Bel)	32 points
5	Bjerre (Den)	29 points
6	Wilkie (GB)	28 points
7	Wim Van Hanegem (Holl)	21 points
8	Spanghero (F)	13 points

550 metres Cycling

1st Heat

Schnabl (Aus)	57.8
Litjens (Holl)	60.0

2nd Heat

Bjerre (Den)	59.5
Van Hanegem (Holl)	62.0

3rd Heat

Bell (Bel)	61.4
Spanghero (F)	67.0

4th Heat

Michanek (Swe)	58.7
Wilkie (GB)	66.8

1st, 2nd place final

1 Michanek	59.0
2 Schnabl	72.4

3rd, 4th place final

1 Bjerre	58.3
2 Litjens	59.4

Overall placings

1 Michanek (Swe)
2 Schnabl (Aus)
3 Bjerre (Den)
4 Litjens (Holl)
5 Bell (Bel) (fastest non-qualifier)

600 metres Steeplechase

1 Bjerre (Den)	1:47.1
2 Bell (Bel)	1:57.8
3 Litjens (Holl)	2:05.0
4 Schnabl (Aus)	2:08.0
5 Van Hanegem (Holl)	2:37.0
6 Wilkie (GB)	2:37.5

*Spanghero, Michanek

Soccer skills

(Goalkeeper Piet Schrijvers Ajax and Holland)

Slalom competition

	Time	Goals
1 Wilkie (GB)	46.80	3
2 Litjens (Holl)	43.23	2
3 Spanghero (F)	51.40	2
4 Michanek (Swe)	53.00	1
5 Bell (Bel)	53.00	0

Penalty Kicks — Goals

1 { Litjens	2
{ Wilkie	2
3 Bell	1
4 Michanek	0
5 Spanhero	0

Overall result

1 Wilkie (GB)
2 Litjens (Holl)
3 Spanghero (F)
4 Bell (Bel)
5 Michanek (Swe)

†Van Hanegem, Bjerre
*Schnabl

Table Tennis

1st round

Bjerre (Den) beat Wilkie (GB)	21-8
Bell (Bel) beat Litjens (Holl)	21-14

Byes

Michanek (Swe) and
Van Hanegem (Holl)

Semi-finals

Bjerre beat Michanek	21-7
Van Hanegem beat Bell	21-11

1st, 2nd place final

Van Hanegem beat Bjerre	21-12

3rd, 4th place final

Bell beat Michanek	21-3

(5th place point to Litjens as highest scoring non-qualifier in 1st round)

*Schnabl, Spanghero

Weightlifting

	Body weight	Weight lifted	Score
1 Schnabl (Aust)	70.0 k	90.0 k	20
2 Bell (Bel)	71.0 k	75.0 k	4
3 Bjerre (Den)	70.0 k	65.0 k	-5
4 Spanghero (F)	102.0 k	95.0 k	-7
5 Van Hanegem (Holl)	82.0 k	70.0 k	-12

*Michanek, Wilkie, Litjens

100 metres
1st Heat
1 Bell (Bel)	12.8
2 Bjerre (Den)	13.3
3 Van Hanegem (Holl)	13.6
4 Michanek (Swe)	13.9

2nd Heat
1 Schnabl (Aus)	13.6
2 Wilkie (GB)	13.9
3 Litjens (Holl)	13.9
4 Spanghero (F)	14.0

Final
1 Litjens	12.0
2 Bell	12.5
3 Schnabl	12.6
4 Van Hanegem	12.8
5 Bjerre	12.9
6 Wilkie	13.3

Shooting (Air Pistols. 8 metres, 5 discs, 20 shots, time limit 5 minutes)
1 Michanek	5 hits, 9 shots, 1:31.0
2 Wilkie	5 hits, 10 shots, 2:11.6
3 Spanghero	5 hits, 19 shots, 4:15.0
4 Schnabl	4 hits, 20 shots, 4:38.0
5 Bjerre	3 hits, 20 shots, 5:00.0
6 Van Hanegem	1 hit, 20 shots, 5:00.0
7 Litjens	0 hits, 20 shots, 5:00.0

*Bell

50 metres Swimming
1 Schnabl (Aus)	37.3
2 Litjens (Holl)	41.3
3 Michanek (Swe)	52.4
4 Bjerre (Den)	57.1
5 Spanghero (F)	1:22

† Wilkie
*Bell
Note: Van Hanegem (Holl) absent, sick.

Gymnasium tests
Parallel Bars Dips
1 Schnabl (Aus)	31
2 Wilkie (GB)	21
3 Spanghero (F)	18
4 Bell (Bel)	17
5 Michanek (Swe)	11

Squat Thrusts
1 Schnabl	73
2 { Bell	66
{ Wilkie	66
4 Michanek	59
5 Spanghero	50

Overall result
1 Schnabl (Aus)
2 Wilkie (GB)
3 Bell (Bel)
4 Spanghero (F)
5 Michanek (swe)

*Bjerre, Van Hanegem, Litjens

125 metres Canoeing (Single kayak) touring canoes)
1st Heat
1 Michanek (Swe)	42.3
2 Schnabl (Aus)	48.2
3 Van Hanegem (Holl)	49.5
4 Litjens (Holl)	50.0

2nd Heat
1 Wilkie (GB)	56.4
2 Bjerre (Den)	63.3
3 Spanghero (F)	68.9
4 Bell (Bel)	1:30.1

Final (Heat winners and two fastest losers)
1 Michanek	41.6
2 Van Hanegem	44.2
3 Wilkie	46.5
4 Schnabl	46.6

(5th place point to Litjens as fastest non-qualifier)

BELGIAN HEAT

Great Britain: Kevin Keegan (Football: Liverpool and England)
France: Marco Ostarcevic (Basketball: Captain Racing Club de France, Yugoslavian born)
Holland: Rudi Krol (Football: Captain of Ajax, World Cup international)
Sweden: Stellan Bengtsson (Table Tennis: triple world champion, 116 caps)
Austria: Franz Klammer (Ski-ing: Olympic champion downhill, World Cup record holder)
Denmark: Ole Ritter (Cycling: world record holder at 5 and 100 metres)
Belgium: Jean-Pierre Coopman (Boxing: national heavyweight champion, fought Muhammad Ali in world title bid)
Gilbert Van Binst (Football: Belgium and Anderlecht captain)

Final result

×1	Kevin Keegan (GB)	54	points
×2	Kroll (Holl)	45½	points
×3	Marco Ostarcevic (F)	45	points
4	Klammer (Aus)	41½	points
5	Van Binst (Bel)	20	points
6	Bengtsson (Swe)	15	points
7	Coopman (Bel)	11	points
8	Ritter (Den)	7	points

100 metres

1	Van Binst (Bel)	11.6
2	Krol (Holl)	11.9
3	Klammer (Aus)	12.4
4	Ostarcevic (F)	12.6
5	Bengtsson (Swe)	13.2
6	Coopman (Bel)	14.2
7	Ritter (Den)	16.0

*Keegan

Soccer skills
Slalom Competition

(1 minute maximum)		Time	Goals
1	Ostarcevic (F)	41.0	1
2	Bengtsson (Swe)	41.2	1
3	Coopman (Bel)	46.5	1
4	Ritter (Den)	expired	1
5	Klammer (Aus)	54.4	0

Penalties		Goals
1	Ostarcevic	4
	⌠ Ritter	2
2	⎨ Klammer	2
	⌡ Bengtsson	2
5	Coopman	0

Overall result

1	Ostarcevic (F)	
2	Bengtsson (Swe)	
3	Ritter (Den)	
4	⌠ Coopman (Bel)	
	⌡ Klammer (Aus)	

†Keegan, Van Binst, Krol

125 metres Canoeing
(Touring single kayaks)

1st heat

1 Klammer (Aus)	47.0
2 Keegan (GB)	47.5
3 Coopman (Bel)	53.2
4 Van Binst (Bel)	64.0

2nd heat

1 Krol (Holl)	50.0
2 Ostarcevic (F)	50.0
3 Bengtsson (Swe)	50.1
4 Ritter (Den)	did not finish

Final
(Heat winners and 2 fastest losers)

1 Keegan	45.5
2 Krol	47.2
3 Klammer	47.2
4 Ostarcevic	did not finish

(Bengtsson (Swe) was awarded the 5th place as the fastest non-qualifier)

Table Tennis

1st round

Van Binst (Bel) bt Ritter (Den)	21-3
Krol (Holl) bt Coopman (Bel)	21-3
Keegan (GB) bt Klammer (Aus)	21-16
Bye	
Ostarcevic	

Semi-finals

Krol beat Van Binst	21-4
Keegan beat Ostarcevic	21-19

3rd, 4th place final

Ostarcevic beat Van Binst	21-12

1st, 2nd place final

Krol beat Keegan	21-7
Klammer	

(highest scoring non-qualifier from 1st round)

†Bengtsson

Weightlifting	Body weight	Weight lifted	Score
1 Keegan (GB)	71.4 k	75.0 k	+3.6
2 Ostarcevic (F)	80.5 k	72.5 k	-8.0 k
3 Bengtsson (Swe)	62.5 k	50.0 k	-12.5
4 Ritter (Den)	79.5 k	60.0 k	-19.5

*Krol, Klammer, Van Binst, Coopman

470 metres Cycling
1st Heat
Klammer (Aus)   43.2
Krol (Holl)
   (did not finish: mechanical failure)
2nd Heat
Coopman (Bel)   47.2
Bengtsson (Swe)   50.0
3rd Heat
Keegan (GB)   fell
Van Binst (Bel)   pulled up
Note: Krol and Van Binst granted re-rides due to malfunctions in heats.
Result
Krol   45.8
Van Binst
   (did not finish: mechanical failure)
Note: Van Binst granted second re-ride. Result (solo ride for time qualification purposes)
Van Binst   50.3
Note: Keegan, injured in fall, granted solo re-ride.
Result
Keegan   45.3
Finals (Fastest two riders to contest 1st and 2nd position)
1 Klammer   43.0
2. Keegan   44.3
3rd, 4th place final
1 Krol   45.7
2 Coopman   46.5
Overall cycle placings
1 Klammer (Aus)
2 Keegan (GB)
3 Krol (Holl)
4 Coopman (Bel)
5 Bengtsson (swe)
   (fastest non-qualifier from heats)

†Ritter
*Ostarcevic

Shooting (9mm FN-Browning Service Pistol, 15 m, 5 shots, maximum score 50)
1	Ostarcevic (F)	37
2	Klammer (Aus)	32
3	Keegan (GB)	28
4 {	Krol (Holl)	27
	Coopman (Bel)	27
6	Van Binst (Bel)	25
7	Ritter (Den)	20
8	Bengtsson (Swe)	16

Gymnasium tests
Parallel Bars Dips
1	Coopman (Bel)	25
2	Klammer (Aus)	20
3	Krol (Holl)	18
4	Keegan (GB)	17
5	Bengtsson (Swe)	16
6	Van Binst (Bel)	11

Squat Thrusts
	Keegan	62
1 {	Klammer	62
	Krol	62
4 {	Van Binst	60
	Coopman	60
6	Bengtsson	45

Overall result
1 Klammer (Aus)
2 Krol (Holl)
3 Coopman (Bel)
4 Keegan (GB)
5 Van Binst (Bel)
6 Bengtsson (Swe)
*Ostarcevic, Ritter

600 metres Steeplechase
1	Kegan (GB)	1:39.8
2	Van Binst (Bel)	1:42.7
3	Klammer (Aus)	1:43.0
4	Krol (Holl)	1:43.1
5	Bengtsson (Swe)	1:45.5
6	Ostarcevic (F)	2:23.1
7	Ritter (Den)	3:08.0

*Coopman

50 metres Swimming: 1 Ostarcevic (F) 35.5. 2 Kroll (Holl) 36.1. 3 Keegan (GB) 39.3. 4 Coopman (Bel) 52.0. 5 Ritter (Den) 57.4. 6 Van Binst (Bel) 1:16.5

*Bengtsson, Klammer

SWEDISH HEAT

Great Britain: David Hemery (Athletics: Olympic gold medallist, UK. 1973 and 1976 Superstar)
Holland: Frank Nusse (Athletics: No. 1 hurdler and Dutch Superstar 1976)
Belgium: François Mathy (Show Jumping: Olympic bronze medallist)
France: Daniel Morelon (Cycling: 5 Olympic medals, 8 world titles, world record holder)
Italy: Marcello Fiasconaro (Athletics: former 800 metres world record holder)
Norway: Sten Stensen (Speed Skating: Olympic 5000 metres gold medallist)
Sweden: Kjell Isaksson (Athletics: three times world pole vault record holder, reigning European Superstar)
Johan Granath (Speed Skating: world champion 500 and 1000 metres)

Final result
×1	Isaksson (Swe)	66	points
×2	Granath (Swe)	42	points
3	David Hemery (GB)	36.33	points
×4	Frank Nusse (Holl)	35.33	points
5	Fiasconaro (I)	27.33	points
6	Stensen (Nor)	22.33	points
7	Mathy (Bel)		
8	Morelon (F)		

100 metres
1	Hemery (GB)	11.6
2	Nusse (Holl)	11.7
3	Isaksson (Swe)	12.0
4	Fiasconaro (I)	12.0
5	Mathy (Bel)	13.4
6	Morelon (F)	14.5

*Stensen, Granath

Soccer skills
(Goalkeeper Jan Nordstrom (IFK))

Slalom Competition		Time	
1	Granath (Swe)	0:42.7	3
2	Stensen (Nor)	1:40.5	1
3	Nursse (Holl)	1:41.3	1
4	Fiasconaro (I)	1:43.0	1
5	Morelon (F)	1:48.0	1
6	Mathy (Bel)	0:56.2	0

Penalties
1	Fiasconaro	5
2 {	Nusse	3
	Morelon	3
	Stensen	3
5	Granath	2
6	Mathy	0

Overall result
1 {	Fiasconaro (I)	
	Stensen (Nor)	
3 {	Granath (Swe)	
	Nusse (Holl)	
5	Morelon (F)	
6	Mathy (Bel)	

*Hemery, Isaksson

125 metres Canoeing
1st Heat
1	Granath (Swe)	45.8
2	Stensen (Nor)	46.9
3	Hemery (GB)	47.2
4	Fiasconaro (I)	55.6

2nd Heat
1	Nusse (Holl)	44.4
2	Isaksson (Swe)	45.8
3	Mathy (Bel)	51.4
4	Morelon (F)	55.5

(Heat winners and two fastest losers qualified for final)

Final
1	Isaksson (Swe)	42.0
2	Granath (Swe)	43.2
3	Nusse (Holl)	45.2
4	Stensen (Nor)	46.0

(5th place awarded to Hemery as fastest non-qualifier)

Table Tennis
1st round
Isaksson beat Hemery	21-8
Granath beat Mathy	21-2
Fiasconaro beat Morelon	21-15
Nusse beat Stensen	21-12

Semi-finals
Isaksson beat Granath	21-12
Nusse beat Fiasconaro	21-11

1st, 2nd place final
Isaksson beat Nusse	21-11

3rd, 4th place final
Granath beat Fiasconaro	21-6

Overall placings
1 Isaksson (Swe)
2 Nusse (Holl)
3 Granath (Swe)
4 Fiasconaro (I)
5 Morelon (F)
  (Highest scoring non-qualifier)

Weightlifting	Body weight	Weight lifted	Score
1 Isaksson (Swe)	70.6 k	105.0 k	34.4 k
2 Granath (Swe)	86.5 k	110.0 k	23.5 k
3 Hemery (GB)	74.8 k	90.0 k	15.2 k
4 Mathy (Bel)	83.0 k	82.5 k	-0.5 k
5 Stensen (Nor)	77.6 k	75.0 k	-2.6 k
6 Morelon (F)	81.0 k	65.0 k	-16.0 k

*Nusse, Fiasconaro

Gymnasium tests
Parallel Bars Dips
1 Hemery (GB) 44
2 Isaksson (Swe) 38
3 Granath (Swe) 28
4 Nusse (Holl) 24
5 Fiasconaro (I) 23
6 Stensen (Nor) 16

Squat Thrusts (1 minute)
1 Isaksson 80
2 Granath 79
3 Hemery 76
4 Nusse 75
5 Stensen 67
6 Fiasconaro 59

(The Referee, after considering a protest by Hemery, increased his score from the 64 given by the assessor to 76)

Overall result
1 Isaksson (Swe)
2 Hemery (GB)
3 Granath (Swe)
4 Nusse (Holl)
5 } Fiasconaro (I)
   } Stensen (Nor)

*Mathy, Morelon

Shooting (.22 FN Browning, 15 metres, 5 shots, maximum 50)
1 Isaksson (Swe) 46
2 { Stensen (Nor) 45
   { Fiasconaro (I) 45
   { Nusse (Holl) 45
5 { Hemery (GB) 44
   { Morelon (F) 44
   { Mathy (Bel) 44
8 Granath (Swe) 43

50 metres Swimming
1 Fiasconaro (I) 29.9
2 Hemery (GB) 31.0
3 Nusse (Holl) 32.3
4 Isaksson (Swe) 33.0
5 Morelon (F) 48.7

*Mathy, Stensen, Granath

500 metres Cycling
1st Heat
(Re-run, following Hemery fall)
Granath (Swe) 44.1
Hemery (GB) 45.3
2nd Heat
Stensen (Nor) 47.1
Mathy (Bel) 49.8
3rd Heat
Nusse (Holl) 48.3
Fiasconaro (I) 51.1
1st, 2nd place final
1 Granath 44.0
2 Hemery 45.1
3rd, 4th place final
1 Nusse 48.10
2 Stensen 48.12

Overall placings
1 Granath (Swe)
2 Hemery (GB)
3 Nusse (Holl)
4 Stensen (Nor)
5 Mathy (Bel) (fastest non-qualifier)

† Morelon
*Isaksson

600 metres Steeplechase
1 Isaksson (Swe) 1:40.4
2 Granath (Swe) 1:41.0
3 Stensen (Nor) 1:50.1
4 Mathy (Bel) 2:08.7
5 Morelon (F) 2:36.2

*Nusse, Hemery, Fiasconaro

FRENCH HEAT

Great Britain: Gareth Edwards (Rugby Union: international and try scoring record holder, British Lion)

Sweden: Bjorn Borg (Lawn Tennis: Wimbledon champion)

Holland: Hennie Kuiper (Cycling: Olympic and Professional champion, Milk Race winner)

Belgium: Ivo Van Damme (Athletics: Olympic silver medal 800 metres and 1500 metres)

Italy: Bruno Arcari (Boxing: former world champion)
   Guiseppe Martinelli (Cycling: Olympic silver medallist)

France: Raymond Poulidor (Cycling: National No. 1 for 16 years)
   Guy Drut (Athletics: Olympic 110 metres gold medallist)

Final result

1	Borg (Swe)	53	points
×2	Drut (F)	45	points
×3	Van Dame (Bel)	44	points
×4	Edwards (GB)	42.5	points
5	Kuiper (Holl)	25.5	points
6	Martinelli (I)	15	points
7	Arcari (I)	10	points
8	Poulidor (F)	3	points

Gymnasium tests

Parallel Bars: Dips

	Dips
Drut	30
Edwards	24
Kuiper	16
Poulidor	14
Van Damme	11
Borg	8
Martinelli	6

Squat Thrusts

Kuiper	82
Edwards	73
Drut	69
Van Damme	69
Martinelli	67
Borg	61
Poulidor	60

Overall result

1	{ Edwards (GB)	
	{ Kuiper (Holl)·	
3	Drut (F)	
4	Van Damme (Bel)	
5	Poulidor (F)	
6	{ Martinelli (I)	
	{ Borg (Swe)	

*Arcari

66 metres Swimming

1	Van Damme (Bel)	1:02.64
2	Martinelli (I)	1:05.37
3	Arcari (I)	1:06.75
4	Kuiper (Holl)	1:29.29

*Edwards, Borg, Poulidor, Drut

Table Tennis

1st round

Edwards beat Arcari	21-6
Van Damme beat Martinelli	21-5
Borg beat Poulidor	21-11
Drut beat Kuiper	21-12

Semi-finals

Edwards beat Van Damme	21-18
Borg beat Drut	21-8

1st, 2nd place final

Borg beat Edwards	21-4

3rd, 4th place final

Van Damme beat Drut	21-14

Overall placings

1 Borg (Swe)
2 Edwards (GB)
3 Van Damme (Bel)
4 Drut (F)
5 Kuiper (Holl)
   (Highest scoring non-qualifier)

100 metres

1st Heat

1	Borg (Swe)	12.3
2	Edwards (GB)	12.6
3	Arcari (I)	22.3

2nd Heat

1	Van Damme (Bel)	14.9
2	Martinelli (I)	15.2
3	Poulidor (F)	15.2

Final (Heat winners and 2 fastest losers)

1 Van Damme
2 Borg
3 Edwards
4 Martinelli
(Poulidor took the point for 5th place as fastest non-qualifier)

†Drut
*Kuiper

Weightlifting

	Body weight	Weight lifted	Score
1 Edwards (GB)	79.6 k	105.0 k	25.4 k
2 Drut (F)	78.3 k	100.0 k	21.7 k
3 Arcari (I)	82.3 k	72.5 k	-9.8 k
4 Martinelli (I)	66.6 k	55.0 k	-11.6 k
5 Poulidor (F)	73.0 k	55.0 k	-18.0 k
6 Kuiper (Holl)	70.6 k	50.0 k	-20.6 k

*Van Damme, Borg

Shooting
(15 metres, .22 unique semi-automatic (except Kuiper and Arcari) .22 FN Browning semi-automatic Kuiper and Arcari left handers. (All competitors 5 shots, maximum score 50)

Note: Kuiper (Holl) and Drut (F) tied with 46 on first shot.

Shoot-off to determine first place
1 Kuiper   47
2 Drut   45

Other placings from first round
3 Edwards (GB)   40
4 Borg (Swe)   39
5 Martinelli (I) 37
6 Van Damme (Bel) 28
7 Arcari (I)   13
8 Poulidor (F)   0

115 metres Canoeing
1 Borg (Swe)   33.15
2 Drut (F)   34.06
3 Edwards (GB)   37.04
4 Kuiper (Holl)   37.20
5 Van Damme (Bel) 42.17
6 Poulidor (F)   58.66

*Arcari, Martinelli

Football
(Goalkeeper Ivan Curkovic, Yugoslavian international of St. Etienne)
Owing to adverse weather conditions, this event was decided only on the Slalom Competition

	Time	
1 Borg (Swe)	37.2	2
2 Van Damme (Bel)	39.4	2
3 Drut (F)	41.8	2
4 Martinelli (I)	54.0	2
5 Edwards (GB)	42.0	1
6 Poulidor (F)	52.0	1
7 Arcari (I)	53.5	1
8 Kuiper (Holl)	46.2	0

Cycling
(Heats 500 m time trials, final 1000 metre pursuit)

1st Heat
Drut (F)   43.00
Van Damme (Bel)   43.20

2nd Heat
Borg (Swe)   51.4
Arcari (I)   66.4

Final
1 Van Damme   1:37.4
2 Drut   1:42.0

Other placings from heat times
3 Borg
4 Arcari

†Poulidor, Kuiper, Martinelli
*Edwards

600 metres Steeplechase
1 Borg (Swe)   1:51.0
2 Drut (F)   1:53.8
3 Edwards (GB)   1:57.6
4 Kuiper (Holl)   2:04.4
5 Martinelli (I)   2:17.5
6 Poulidor (F)   2:23.0
Arcari (I)   did not finish

†Van Damme

EUROPEAN SUPERSTARS FINAL 1976 Qualifications for final

Two competitors from each of the nations who have taken part in every heat (Belgium, Great Britain, France, Holland and Sweden).
One competitor from the "floating" nations (Austria, Germany, Norway, Denmark, Switzerland and Italy).
Finalists to be heat winners or highest points scorers from each nation.
Highest points scorer from floating nations.
Note: Kevin Keegan (Belgian heat winner) and Bjorn Borg (French heat winner) were unable to accept places in the final due to outstanding committments.

1976 Finalists (11)
Great Britain: John Conteh (Boxing: British heat winner)
 Gareth Edwards (Rugby Union: 4th place, French heat 42.5 points)
Austria: Karl Schnabl (Ski Jumping: Dutch heat winner)
Belgium: OLIN 'Corky' Bell (Basketball: equal 3rd Dutch heat, 32 points)
 Ivo Van Damme (Athletics: 3rd French heat, 44 points)
France: Guy Drut (Athletics: 2nd French heat, 45 points)
 Marco Ostarcevic (Basketball: 3rd Belgian heat, 45 points)
Holland: Rudi Krol (Football: 2nd Belgian heat, 45 ½ points)
 Frank Nusse (Athletics: 4th Swedish heat, 35.33 points)
Sweden: Johan Granath (Speed Skating: 2nd Swedish heat, 42 points)
 Kjell Isaksson (Athletics: winner Swedish heat, 66 points)

Scoring system: Winner 10 points, 2nd 8 points, 3rd 6 points, 4th 4 points, 5th 2 points, 6th 1 point.

Final result

1	Isaksson (Swe)	68 points	$10,000
2	Granath (Swe)	48 points	$5,000
	Schanbl (Aus)	48 points	$5,000
4	Nusse (Holl)	38 points	$3,000
5	Krol (Holl)		24 points
6	Edwards (GB)		20 points
	(only four events)		
7	Drut (F)		16 points
8	Bell (Bel)		14 points
9	Conteh (GB)		13 points
10	Van Damme (Bel)		12 ½ points
11	Ostarcevic (F)		8 ½ points

50 metres Swimming
1	Ostarcevic	35.1
2	Nusse	35.8
3	Krol	37.2
4	Van Damme	53.1

2nd Heat
1	Isaksson	34.2
2	Schnabl	36.8
3	Drut	40.4

Final (Heat winners and three fastest losers)
1	Isaksson (Swe)	32.5
2	Nusse (Holl)	33.2
3	Ostarcevic (F)	33.3
4	Schnabl (Aus)	36.0
5	Krol (Holl)	38.2

(6˙Drut (F) fastest non-qualifier)
*Conteh, Bell, Granath, Edwards

Soccer skills
(Goalkeeper: Peter Atjanski, Eindhoven)

Slalom test
		Time	
1	Edwards	40.9	3 goals
2	Van Damme	43.0	1 goal
3	Ostarcevic	46.8	1 goal
4	Conteh	52.8	1 goal
5	Bell	55.6	1 goal
6	Granath	48.0	0 goal
7	Nusse	48.2	0 goal
8	Drut	55.1	0 goal

Penalties (5 attempts)
1	Nusse	4 goals
	Drut	4 goals
3	Edwards	3 goals
	Bell	3 goals
5	Granath	2 goals
	Conteh	2 goals
7	Ostarcevic	1 goal
8	Van Damme	0 goal

Overall placings
1	Edwards (GB)	
2	Bell (Bel)	
	Nusse (Holl)	
4	Drut (F)	
	Conteh (GB)	
6	Van Damme (Bel)	
	Ostarcevic (F)	
8	Granath (Swe)	

†Krol *Isaksson, Schnabl

Weightlifting

	Body weight	Weight lifted	Score
1 Isaksson (Swe)	70.6 k	105.0 k	34.4 k
2 Granath (Swe)	88.0 k	115.0 k	27.0 k
3 Schnabl (Aus)	73.5 k	100.0 k	26.5 k
4 Edwards (GB)	79.2 k	100.0 k	20.8 k
5 Drut (F)	80.8 k	95.0 k	14.2 k
6 Conteh (GB)	82.8 k	95.0 k	12.2 k
7 Ostarcevic (F)	80.2 k	75.0 k	-5.2 k
8 Bell (Bel)	73.5 k	60.0 k	-13.5 k

*Van Damme, Krol, Nusse

100 metres
1st Heat
1 Krol	12.0
2 Ostarcevic	12.5
3 Conteh	12.6
4 Bell	12.6

2nd Heat
1 Van Damme	11.7
2 Nusse	11.8
3 Isaksson	11.9
4 Schnabl	12.4

Final (Heat winners and four fastest losers)
1 Van Damme (Bel)	11.5
2 Nusse (Holl)	11.5
3 Isaksson (Swe)	11.8
4 Krol (Holl)	11.8
5 Schnabl (Aus)	12.5
6 Ostarcevic (F)	12.8

†Drut
*Granath
Note: Edwards (GB) absent through illness

600 metres Steeplechase
1 Granath (Swe)	1:46.6
2 Isaksson (Swe)	1:47.7
3 Schnabl (Aus)	1:50.6
4 Krol (Holl)	1:55.5
5 Drut (F)	1:55.9
6 Bell (Bel)	1:56.2
7 Conteh (GB)	2:01.1
†Edwards	Absent ill

† Van Damme
*Ostarcevic, Nusse

Gymnasium tests
Parallel Bars Dips
Schnabl (Aus)	53
Isaksson (Swe)	48
Drut (F)	33
Granath (Swe)	32
Conteh (GB)	31
Nusse (Holl)	23
Krol (Holl)	22
Van Damme (Bel)	12
Bell (Bel)	11

Squat Thrusts
Isaksson	86
Conteh	85
Schnabl	82
Nusse	82
Granath	75
Bell	61
Drut	60
Van Damme	52
Krol	43

Overall gynasium placings
1	Isaksson (Swe)	
2	Schnabl (Aus)	
3	Conteh (GB)	
4	Granath (Swe)	
5	Nusse (Holl)	
6	Drut (F)	
7	Bell (Bel)	
8	Van Damme (Bel)	
	Krol (Holl)	
Edwards (GB)		absent ill

*Ostarcevic

Table Tennis
Qualifying Match
Edwards beat Van Damme	21-15

1st round
Krol beat Granath	21-13
Bell beat Conteh	21-6
Isaksson beat Nusse	21-14
Edwards beat Ostarcevic	21-19

Semi-finals
Krol beat Bell	21-9
Isaksson beat Edwards	21-3

1st, 2nd place final
Isaksson beat Krol	21-17

3rd, 4th place final
Edwards beat Bell	21-14

5th, 6th place final
Nusse beat Ostarcevic	21-18

Overall placings
1 Isaksson (Swe)
2 Krol (Holl)
3 Edwards (GB)
4 Bell (Bel)
5 Nusse (Holl)
6 Ostarcevic (F)

*Schnabl, Drut

125 metres Canoeing
1st Heat
1	Drut	45.6
2	Conteh	45.7
3	Nusse	46.6
4	Ostarcevic	50.1
5	Van Damme	58.2

2nd Heat
1	Isaksson	41.1
2	Granath	44.2
3	Schnabl	46.0
4	Krol	50.2

Final (Heat winners and three fastest losers)
1	Isaksson (Swe)	41.4
2	Granath (Swe)	44.1
3	Drut (F)	47.2
4	Schnabl (Aus)	50.5
5	Conteh (GB)	52.1

(6th Nusse (Holl), fastest non-qualifier)

*Bell
Note: Edwards absent ill

800 metres Cycling
1st Heat (Time trials)
Drut (F)	1:06.8
Bell (Bel)	1:07.4

2nd Heat
Granath (Swe)	1:02.2
Krol (Holl)	1:05.8

3rd Heat
Schnabl (Aus)	1:02.9
Nusse (Holl)	1:04.3

4th Heat
Van Damme (Bel)	1:06.4
Ostarcevic (F)	1:14.1

Match races (from heat times)
1st, 2nd place final
1	Granath	1:00.0
2	Schnabl	1:12.5

3rd, 4th place final
3	Krol	1:03.8
4	Nusse	1:03.9

5th, 6th place final
5	Van Damme	1:04.8
6	Drut	1:26.0

*Isaksson, Edwards

Shooting (8 metres, 5 clay discs, 20 shots, 5 minutes Air-pistol)

		Shots	Kills	Time	Points
1	Schnabl (Aus)	8	5	1:55	91
2	Granath (Swe)	9	5	1:56	88
3	Nusse (Holl)	11	5	2:02	82
4	Isaksson (Swe)	13	5	2:40	76
5	Bell (Bel)	14	5	2:50	73
6	Conteh (GB)	17	5	3:45	64
7	Edwards (GB)	19	5	4:59	58
8	Drut (F)	20	4	4:09	44
9	Ostarcevic (F)	20	4	4:35	44
10	Krol (Holl)	20	2	4:15	22
11	Van Damme (Bel)	19	2	5:00	19
	(time expired)				

WORLD SUPERSTARS CHAMPIONSHIP March 15-16 1977.
Calloway Gardens, Pine Mountain, Georgia, U.S.A.

Competitors (15)
Great Britain: John Conteh and Gareth Edwards
Holland: Rudi Krol and Frank Nusse
Austria: Karl Schnabl
Belgium: 'Corky' Bell
Canada: Tony Gabriel (Professional football: Canadian Superstar champion)
France: Guy Drut
New Zealand: Peter Snell (Athletics: triple Olympic gold medallist 800 and 1500 metres, New Zealand Superstars champion)
Sweden: Kjell Isaksson
United States: Dave Casper
Billie 'White Shoes' Johnson
Jim Taylor
Lynn Swann
(all American pro football stars)
Bob Seagren (Athletics: Olympic gold medallist and former world record holder, pole vaulting, first US Superstar champion)
Prize money: 300 US dollars for every point won
Bonus: champion 25,000 US dollars, runner-up $15,000, 3rd $10,000, 4th $5,000, 5th $3,000, 6th $2,000.
Ten events, each competitor chooses seven, (barred from speciality), 10 points for win, 7 for second, then 4, 2, 1.

Final result

World Superstars champion:	Bob Seagren (US)	40.0 points	$37,000
Runner-up:	Kjell Isaksson (Swe)	32.0 points	$24,600
3:	Peter Snell (NZ)	30.0 points	$19,000
4:	Lynn Swann (US)	20.5 points	$11,150
5:	Dave Casper (US)	18.0 points	$8,400
6:	Frank Nusse (Hol)	17.8 points	$7,340
7:	Billy Johnson (US)	15.8 points	$4,740
8:	Jim Taylor (US)	14.8 points	$4,440
9:	Guy Drut (F)	14.0 points	$4,200
10:	Karl Schnabl (Aus)	9.5 points	$2,850
11:	Rudi Krol (Hol)	8.0 points	$2,400
12:	Corky Bell (Bel)	7.0 points	$2,100
13:	Gareth Edwards (GB)	4.8 points	$1,440
14:	Tony Gabriel (Can)	4.0 points	$1,200
15:	John Conteh (GB)	3.8 points	$1,140

Weightlifting (jerk overhead only, no body weight equalising formula)

1	Casper (US)	270 lbs
2	Isaksson (Swe)	265 lbs
3	Taylor (US)	260 lbs
4	Swann (US)	240 lbs
	Schnabl (Aus)	240 lbs
6	Drut (F)	230 lbs
7	Conteh (GB)	220 lbs
	Gabriel (Can)	220 lbs
9	Edwards (GB)	210 lbs
	Johnson (US)	210 lbs
11	Nusse (Hol)	200 lbs

Half-mile (track)

1	Seagren (US)	2:08.70
2	Bell (Bel)	2:10.43
3	Gabriel (Can)	2:13.30
4	Schnabl (Aus)	2:15.00
5	Conteh (GB)	2:17.48

Did not finish:
Krol, Swann, Johnson, Drut

Did not start: Edwards (GB)

Gymnasium tests

(Two-part competition consisting of chin-ups where competitor hangs at arms length from overhead bar and then pulls himself up until chin is above bar, repeating as often as possible in one minute; then standard parallel bars dips but for only one minute. Scores added together to determine final result.)

		Chins	Dips	Total
1	Isaksson (Swe)	33	47	80
2	Seagren (US)	28	46	74
3	Schnabl (Aus)	27	34	61
4	Johnson (US)	27	24	51
5	Swann (US)	25	25	50
6	Conteh (GB)	16	33	49
7	Edwards (GB)	22	24	46
8	Snell (NZ)	16	—	16
9	Bell (Bel)	15	—	15
10	Casper (US)	12	—	12
11	Taylor (US)	9	—	9

Football penalties (5 attempts)

(Goalkeeper Paul Hammond, Tampa Bay Rowdies, ex Crystal Palace)
Tie breaker used to decide result after 6 competitors scored 4 goals each.

1	Drut (F)	5
	Conteh (GB)	4
	Edwards (GB)	4
2	Taylor (US)	4
	Nusse (Hol)	4
	Johnson (Hol)	4
7	Casper (US)	2
	Swann (US)	1
8	Snell (NZ)	1
	Gabriel (Can)	1
11	Bell (Bel)	0

Swimming (heats 50 metres, final 100 metres. Heat winners and next 3 fastest into final)

1st heat

1	Isaksson (Swe)	28.80
2	Schnabl (Aus)	30.90
3	Krol (Hol)	31.21
4	Drut (F)	31.75

2nd heat

1	Casper (US)	27.34
2	Seagren (US)	27.88
3	Nusse (Hol)	28.31

Final

1	Seagren	59.95
2	Casper	1:04.10
3	Nusse	1:05.09
4	Isaksson	1:06.00
5	Schnabl	1:35.35

Cycle race (Heats half mile, final 1 1/3 miles, heat winners and next three fastest into final)

1st heat

1	Krol (Hol)	1:10.70
2	Isaksson (Swe)	1:10.95
3	Schnabl (Aus)	1:11.40
4	Gabriel (US)	1:20.26

2nd heat

1	Snell (NZ)	1:02.90
2	Seagren (US)	1:13.00
3	Nusse (Hol)	1:13.33
4	Taylor (US)	1:13.60

Final

1	Snell	3:12.60
2	Isaksson	3:18.28
3	Krol	3:18.59
4	Seagren	3:18.60
5	Schnabl	(did not finish)

Obstacle race

1	Swann (US)	24.21
2	Seagren (US)	24.64
3	Drut (F)	24.84
4	Isaksson (Swe)	25.81
5	Johnson (US)	26.20
6	Schnabl (Aus)	29.20
	Snell (NZ)	29.20
8	Nusse (Hol)	29.52
9	Gabriel (Can)	34.23
10	Krol (Hol)	40.69
11	Conteh (GB)	41.81
12	Casper (US)	(did not finish)

Taylor (US) and Bell (Bel) scratched

100 yards (Heat winners and next 3 fastest to final)

1st heat

1	Johnson (US)	10.29
2	Swann (US)	10.45
3	Casper (US)	10.65
4	Seagren (US)	10.80
5	Conteh (GB)	11.81

2nd heat

1	Krol (Hol)	10.66
2	Snell (NZ)	11.00
3	Edwards (GB)	11.28
4	Bell (Bel)	11.30

Final

1	Johnson	9.90
2	Swann	10.27
3	Krol	10.39
4	Seagren	10.40
5	Casper	10.86

Rowing (2 fastest from time trials to head-to head final)

Time trials

Casper (US) 40.25 beat Edwards (GB) 42.31

Taylor (US) 38.66 beat Krol (Hol) 39.76

Schnabl (Aus) 38.84 beat Conteh (GB) 41.11

Nusse (Hol) 38.31 beat Snell (NZ) 38.42

Gabriel (Can) 42.37 beat Drut (F) 42.86

Isaksson (Swe) 38.51 beat Seagren (US) 38.64

Final

Snell beat Nusse

Final rowing placings

1 Snell
2 Nusse
3 Isaksson
4 Seagren
5 Taylor

Lawn Tennis

1st round

Nusse (Hol) bt Bell (Bel)	6-1
Krol (Hol) bt Isaksson (Swe)	6-0
Edwards (GB) bt Gabriel (Can)	6-1

2nd round

Nusse (Hol) bt Swann (US)	6-4
Taylor (US) bt Krol (Hol)	6-0
Edwards (GB) bt Drut (F)	6-0
Snell (NZ) bt Johnson (US)	6-2

Semi-finals

Taylor bt Nusse	6-4
Snell bt Edwards	6-1

Final

Snell bt Taylor	6-4

Final tennis placings

1 Snell
2 Taylor
3 Nusse
4 Edwards
5 Swann

48 JOHANNESSEN–FISCHER
OLYMPIAD, HAVANA 1966

Benkö Gambit Declined

(by transposition)

1 P—Q4, N—KB3; 2 N—KB3, P—B4;
3 P—Q5, P—QN4 ?!; 4 P—B4, B—N2;
5 P—KN3
Also good for White is 5 QN—Q2, e.g.
5...P×P; 6 P—K4, P—K3; 7 P×P,
BP×P; 8 P—K5 !, and 9 N×P.
    5...P—N3; 6 B—N2, P×P; 7 N—
B3, B—N2; 8 O—O, O—O; 9 N—
K5, P—Q3; 10 N×QBP, QN—Q2;
11 R—K1, B—QR3
Now that Black has completed his
development he prepares for action on
the QN file.
    12 Q—R4, Q—B1
Black can also play 12...B×N; 13
Q×B, R—N1, with some initiative, but
Fischer has other ideas – he has already
calculated the consequences of White's
sixteenth move.
    13 N—R5, N—N3; 14 Q—R4, R—
K1; 15 B—N5
Intending to intensify his pressure
against K7.
    15...Q—B2; 16 N—B6, B—N2; 17
P—K4, N(N3)—Q2
Not 17...B×N; 18 P×B, Q×P ?; 19
P—K5, N(B3)—Q4; 20 N×N, N×N;
21 P—K6 !, and Black's Q4 knight will
soon be lost.
    18 P—B4, K—R1
A dual purpose move, vacating KN1 as
a retreat square for his KN, and ensuring
that if White ever plays N×KP (or
N—K7) it will not be with check.
    19 P—K5 !
Otherwise comes 19...N—KN1, when
White's QB is doing nothing.
    19...P×P; 20 P×P ?
After 20 N×P(K5) ! White still has some
advantage, e.g. 20...K—N1; 21 N—
B6 !, or 20...N×N; 21 P×N, N—

Q2; 22 P—K6, P×P; 23 R×P, B—
KB3; 24 QR—K1. Probably Fischer
missed 20 N×P when analysing his
twelfth move. Now the game ends in a
hurricane.

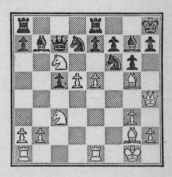

    20...N×QP !; 21 N×N
No better is 21 B×N, B×N; 22 B×BP,
N×P; 23 R×N, Q×R; 24 B×NP, Q—
Q5 ch.
    21...Q×N
Now we see why it is important for
Black's king to be away from KN1.
    22 P—K6, N—K4 !
If 22...P×P; 23 N—B4, threatening
24 N×NP ch.
    23 R×N
After 23 P×P, R—KB1; 24 B×P,
R×P, Black has a tremendous game.
    23...B×R; 24 P×P, R—KB1
Threatening 25...B—Q5 ch; 26 K—R1,
Q×N !
    25 P—KR3, R×P; 26 N—B4, R×N !;
27 Resigns
Since 27 B×Q, R×Q; 28 B×B, R×P;
29 B×R, R×P ch, leaves Black three
pawns ahead in the endgame, and
27...B—Q5 ch; 28 K—N2, R—B7 ch;
29 K—N1, B×B, is also not without its
points.

In 1967 Fischer lost three games (out of thirty-six), two of them to Geller. He had also lost to Geller on their previous meeting (the 1965 Capablanca Memorial Tournament) and up to the time of writing Geller leads in their individual contest by five wins to three with two draws. Probably the trouble was stylistic – Geller too, likes to play positions where his opponent has little or no counterplay. But part of the problem was certainly psychological.

49 FISCHER–GELLER
MONACO 1967

Sicilian Defence

1 P—K4, P—QB4; 2 N—KB3, P—Q3; 3 P—Q4, P×P; 4 N×P, N—KB3; 5 N—QB3, P—QR3; 6 B—KN5, P—K3; 7 P—B4, Q—N3!

That's not fair, that's my line.

8 Q—Q2, Q×P; 9 R—QN1, Q—R6; 10 P—B5

Avoiding the critical lines starting with 10 P—K5. Some commentators claimed that this was because Fischer was already assured of first place and didn't want to give away any free information. But I cannot believe that anyone who is so devoted to the game would wilfully play what he considered to be an inferior move.

10...N—B3; 11 P×P, P×P; 12 N×N, P×N; 13 P—K5, N—Q4?

At the time this game was played it was thought that 13...P×P; 14 B×N, P×B; 15 N—K4, was crushing for White, but Fischer reversed this opinion a few months later in his game with Kavalek from the Sousse Interzonal (page 106).

14 N×N, BP×N; 15 B—K2!, P×P; 16 O—O, B—B4 ch; 17 K—R1, R—B1; 18 P—B4, R×R ch; 19 R×R, B—N2

Probably stronger is 19...P—R3! so that after 20 B—R4 Black can play 20...P—N4 to kill White's play on the dark squares. After 19...P—R3, the game might continue 20 B—R5 ch, K—Q2; 21 P×P, P×B; 22 P×P dbl ch,

K—B2; 23 Q—Q5, R—R2; 24 B—B3 R—N2, and White's attack soon peters out.

20 B—N4?

This natural move loses almost immediately. After the game Fischer maintained that 20 Q—B2 would have won and indeed Tal employed this move in a brilliancy a few months later: (20 Q—B2), P—K5 (better is 20...P—N3; 21 B—N4, B—QB1, and if 22 Q—Q2, Q—N5; or 22 Q—Q1, B—K2. According to O'Kelly the best defence is 20... B—K2; 21 Q×P, B×B; 22 Q—R5 ch, K—Q2; 23 Q×B, K—Q3; 24 Q×NP, R—QN1); 21 B—N4, B—K2; 22 Q—B2, O—O—O; 23 B—B4!, B—Q3; 24 B×P ch, K—N1; 25 Q—N6!, B×B; 26 Q×R ch, K—R2; 27 R—QN1, Q—Q3; 28 B×P!, B×B; 29 Q×Q, B×Q; 30 P×B, Resigns. Tal–Bogdanovic,